Dead Leaves

Dead Leaves
Two Years in the Rhodesian War

Dan Wylie

University of Natal Press
Pietermaritzburg
2002

Dead Leaves: Two Years in the Rhodesian War

ISBN 1 86914 005 2

Published by University of Natal Press
Private Bag X01
Scottsville 3209
South Africa
E-mail: books@nu.ac.za

Editor: Andrea Nattrass
Typesetter: Trish Comrie

Cover photograph by John McKinnell
Camouflage shirt courtesy of Norbert Draeger
Maps by Maurise Bauer

Printed and bound by Interpak Books, Pietermaritzburg

This book is dedicated to my parents, who never wavered.

Overview of Rhodesia, 1978–79.

Contents

Author's note

Although this account is fairly closely autobiographical, no one is likely to recognise themselves in these pages. My companions in this experience have been fictionalised out of all recognition. With the exception of Dr Oliver Ransford and various authors, all names have been changed, and no accurate portrayal of any real person living or dead is intended.

I have preserved place-names as they were in 1978–79. Salisbury is now Harare; Gwelo now Gweru; Norton now Chegutu; Umtali now Mutare; Fort Victoria now Masvingo; Wankie now Hwange; and Chipinga now Chipinge. Similarly, my use of disparaging terms for black people or for guerrilla fighters is intended to reflect our usage then, not my attitude now.

Christina, Don, Kevin and Nikki have all helped to refine the book into what it is, and to them I am especially grateful. My editor Andrea Nattrass has been, as always, wonderfully perceptive and dedicated.

Foreword

The last years of Rhodesia (from 1972 until 1980) were not only years of war but were complicated by the demands of the opposing discourses of empire and nationalism. The proponents of empire claim that their social arts give proportion and measure to raw nature; their civilisation will contain savagery. While empire homogenises diverse peoples by allowing them access to its allegedly superior wisdom, it modifies provincialism by allowing the merely local to glimpse possibilities in the global and the cosmopolitan. Nationalism, by contrast, affirms homogeneity by claiming for a people a shared past and a common future. It valorises as a significant centre what empire saw as marginal, and argues that the values of the metropole are irrelevant to its character as nation. While empire relocates the colony in an imperial history constructed out of imperial narratives, the colony on the cusp of nationhood recovers memories that owe nothing to the imperial past. Refusing its character as artless and random, the nation knows itself through narratives of control that anticipate progress and purpose outside of empire.

When the metropole is European and the new nation African or Asian, diverse geographical and racial groundings make different pasts and different destinies obvious. Southern Rhodesia's whites lacked this grace of perceptible difference. The majority had been in the country only since the early 1950s and they inherited the space created by the pioneers rather than being their literal descendants. Whether as pioneers or post-war immigrants, Rhodesians had played their role in helping to add further dimensions to Britain's imperial and national character. However much they disliked the idea, Rhodesians were almost but not quite British.

This tension between colony and nation can be seen in Ian Smith's unilateral declaration of independence (UDI) speech in 1965. The proclamation of independence consciously echoes the United States's declaration of independence: 'Whereas in the course of human affairs history has shown that it may become necessary for a people to resolve their political affiliations . . .'. On the one hand, in his speech after issuing the proclamation, Smith used the past to give Rhodesians discrete national identity: 'we are a courageous people and history has cast us in an heroic role'. On the other hand, Smith's claim that UDI was striking a blow 'for the preservation of justice, civilisation and Christianity' was not an expression of nationalism but a claim authorised by empire. Empire as one ideology behind UDI is also discernible in Smith's professions of Rhodesians' 'loyalty to the Crown and to their kith and kin in the United Kingdom and elsewhere'. This double consciousness of identities national and imperial was to muddle the rhetoric of the next fifteen violent years. Sometimes these conflicting demands were reconciled through a curious dialectic. Smith and his supporters both inside and outside Rhodesia claimed that Rhodesia, in taking command of its national destiny, was realising British values that Britain had betrayed by, as Smith said, its 'surrender' to 'communists in the Afro-Asian bloc'.

Part of Dan Wylie's considerable achievement in *Dead Leaves* is to create a narrative that acknowledges and accommodates these competing discourses. The reminiscences of the main narrative are in part a commentary on his own writings, principally the entries from the diaries that Wylie kept through the years of his national service. Wylie was six at UDI and his diaries show an independence of thought and attitude battling with a teenager's need to conform to whatever his peers were thinking. As a serviceman, conformity was demanded to the narrow nationalism imagined by the Rhodesia Front and which censorship had re-enforced since UDI. The wisdom of hindsight does not render infallible the larger narrative, however. 'But what *is* my own voice?' Wylie asks, exasperated by the knowledge that the voice of his diary is a conscious imitation of Hopkins's journals. Later this becomes, 'Who am I writing for?' Nationalism and empire compete for attention. At Heany Junction, the station for Llewellin Barracks, he remembers that Selous had said that Heany, a Virginian adventurer, showed the qualities that had 'already won half the world for the Anglo-Saxon race'. Wylie comments ironically: 'It is the heritage of that race which, stumbling sleepily from our train, we are about to begin to fight for.' He and his fellow recruits were about to awake into recognition of a world more complex than the one which the Rhodesian propaganda machine had created where obvious righteousness confronted obvious evil.

Wylie is conscious of his book's inter-textual dimensions, appropriating, adding to and subverting the narratives of Rhodesian nationalism. The anaesthetist at an operation for Wylie's hand smashed during the first weeks of training is Oliver Ransford, whose book *The Rulers of Rhodesia* the nineteen-year-old Wylie has read and admired. Ransford argued that élites have always ruled the country and the British South Africa Company's successful occupation of 1890 was not a disjunction of indigenous history but confirmation of Africa's need for authority. In the late 1960s and 70s, Books of Rhodesia republished early books on the country written by pre-colonial travellers, hunters and missionaries as well as the early settlers and administrators. An older Wylie writes that subscribing to the series then felt like 'a mild act of patriotism' but, typically, he immediately complicates patriotism. Books of Rhodesia provides 'unlimited justification for current attitudes', which is the function of any text used to preserve memories for the nation. As an illustration, he quotes Hans Sauer's confident attribution of Great Zimbabwe to the Phoenicians because blacks have smaller brains than whites. Another text is Wylie's 'leatherbound, numbered-and-signed, limited edition copy' of *Shadows of War*, an extraordinary book of pencil sketches of Rhodesia at war interspersed with quotations from Rhodesian poets. Both sketches and poems affect to confront with honesty a war in which, as Wylie remarks, 'Ordinary men [are] absorbed in mayhem.' But the formal competence of pencil and poem refuses any possibility of mayhem edging into chaos and the men in the sketches are not ordinary. Beneath grime and exhaustion and thirst their beauty and strength are idealised, a reassurance of a secure future. The 'lush format' of the book, Wylie writes, 'seems already weighty with anticipatory nostalgia'. Nostalgia is not memory but memory which has excised misery, pain, and boredom and which refuses the guilt of criminality. *Dead Leaves* confronts the evasions of *Shadows of War*: 'I cannot indulge in nostalgia yet. I have not been released from the violent circle of the inferno.'

* * *

Although there had been earlier incursions and contacts, the Zimbabwean war began with the ZANLA attacks on farms in the north-east in December 1972. The Rhodesians could have repulsed these and the ZIPRA incursions further west almost indefinitely, but the anti-colonial coup in Portugal in April 1974 opened the sixteen-hundred-kilometre Rhodesia–Mozambique border to ZANLA attacks. This new front stretched the Rhodesian army to its limit. The South African government's response to the independence of Mozambique and Angola was to initiate a détente with Zambia using Rhodesia as a bargaining chip. In August 1974, without telling Smith beforehand what he intended to do, Vorster, at Kaunda's request, withdrew several South African police details who were helping to patrol the northern border. During the next six months, without warning, for days at a time the South Africans would withhold ammunition supplies from the Rhodesians. No action could more forcibly remind Rhodesia of the realities of power in the sub-region. South African pressure forced the Rhodesian regime in November 1974 to release the leaders of the two principal nationalist parties some of whom had been in detention since 1962 and who, as soon as they were released, crossed the border. This should have signalled the end of the war but ZAPU and more particularly ZANU were weakened by factionalism based on regionalism, class and ethnicity that erupted in fighting in both Zambia and Mozambique. In March 1975, Herbert Chitepo the ZANU external chairman was assassinated. Although it is now claimed that the Rhodesians were his killers, at the time the Commission set up by the Organisation of African Unity to investigate his murder blamed a powerful faction in ZANU for the event and several ZANU leaders were subsequently detained in Zambia. In 1976, in an attempt to address factionalism, ZANU and ZAPU had formed an alliance called the Patriotic Front and the guerrilla armies fought under this title until Zimbabwean independence. The detention of ZANU leaders worked to Robert Mugabe's advantage, as there were few politicians with sufficient influence to oppose him as he consolidated his authority over ZANU. In 1977 at Chimoio in Mozambique, he was elected ZANU President and Commander-in-Chief of ZANLA. Mugabe succeeded in unifying the squabbling party and the Patriotic Front became a more effective fighting force than they had been since the fighting began.

The political pressures on Smith continued to build up. Henry

Kissinger, the American Secretary of State, had promised to support South African attacks on Angola in return for South Africa's backing of a settlement in Rhodesia. In September 1976, at a meeting with Kissinger and Smith, Vorster made his government's position clear: Rhodesia could no longer rely on South Africa financially or militarily. For two years, there was a seemingly endless succession of delegations and meetings as Smith tried to create various alliances with nationalist leaders, both inside and outside Zimbabwe, that the British government would accept. Only in 1978, however, and without British backing, did he finally reach a compromise with Bishop Muzorewa. Another significant political development became more obvious during 1977. Without South African backing, the war seemed an exercise in futility and whites began to question their future in Rhodesia. There was a massive emigration by families whose lives were interrupted by constant call-ups and whose men had no desire to spend the rest of their lives patrolling the increasingly dangerous borders. In his New Year's speech for 1978, Smith acknowledged for the first time that his principal political objective was to retain white confidence and stem the flow of emigration. The speech showed just how far he had travelled from the portentous demand in 1965 that the nation be allowed to realise its historic destiny. By 'nation' he meant whites – and they were now showing a singular lack of commitment to their history by simply leaving. Now he sought no more than 'safeguards which will ensure that a future Government will not be able to abuse its power by resorting to actions which are dishonest or immoral'. A 'justiceable Bill of Rights to protect the rights and freedoms of individuals' would prevent such an abuse of power – a curious expectation from a man who for the previous fourteen years had governed under a state of emergency and who had with UDI thrown all constitutions aside. Three days after Smith made this speech Dan Wylie arrived at Llewellin Barracks.

* * *

The futility of war is a convention in the reminiscences of many soldiers. In 1978, a sense of futility was a sensible response to a war that Wylie soon realised was 'unwinnable'. In March 1978, Smith, Abel Muzorewa and Chief Chirau signed the settlement which made way for Zimbabwe-Rhodesia, 'one-man-one-vote' and abolished everything the Rhodesians claimed they were fighting for. In May 1979, with the elections completed, the Rhodesian Parliament was dissolved and Muzorewa became Prime Minister. Ninety years of white rule had ended. Wylie's national service was punctuated by these moments from the larger context although their implications hardly impinged on what he was doing. '"[T]he big moral picture [is] confused,"' Wylie is told when he is about to embark on a terrifying mission into the Chungwe Valley. And his companion goes on: '"The Buddha said, 'There is only the moment.'"' In this context, the moment involves no other moral imperative than 'kill or be killed'. Fighting for the sovereignty of one's nation is reduced to killing people who want to kill those, black or white, that history has put on your side. With singular honesty, Wylie records the two contacts in which he kills people. The killings are morally indefensible in the ordinary context in which most of us live out our lives. But the context of those last two years before Zimbabwean independence was so extraordinary that the reader too suspends moral judgement. Wylie shows how the army conditions his reflexes so that no scruple can interfere with action. Likewise, the reader – experiencing each moment in Wylie's narrative as possessing its own imperatives – trusts the authority of the moment for making him act as he does.

Throughout *Dead Leaves*, Wylie grasps for something positive that he can take from his two years of National Service. In an essay he wrote at the time, he claims that what you learn in the army is a wisdom drawn from the experience of paradox: '[the] sad-eyed businessman killing for his life, bloody corpses in a spectacular landscape, ribald jokes in the middle of a contact'. When he wrote this, however, he had not been involved in a 'contact' and the older Wylie remarks that his younger self 'want[ed] to be experienced without having suffered the pain'. This particular essay, the writing of the younger man, contains the seminal idea of the book. Paradox is 'more valuable to the soldier than to the human being', he confidently proclaims. But the problem is, he adds, that 'the soldier and human being are one and the same, and one inevitably creeps over on the other'.

Each one of us is a public and a private person, and both are manifestations of our humanity that history has created. No individual can stand outside history and the history of whites in Rhodesia created the soldier to defend a racially exclusive nationalism as much as it created the guerrillas making their own claims to nationhood. But the same history created the Dan Wylie who experiences the beauties of the Zambezi Valley, the Matopos and the mountains along the Mozambique border not as something exotic but as his familiar reality. Perhaps the most important part of our humanity is our capacity to question both our public and private selves, and how honestly they confront our experiences. This task *Dead Leaves* superbly achieves by rehearsing the language and narratives that have formed competing memories and setting them against other public narratives, the official histories of this period. The experience the book confronts of a white fighting for the indefensible emerges more morally complex than we may have thought possible.

Anthony Chennells

As time went by our need to fight for the ideal increased to an unquestioning possession, riding with spur and rein over our doubts. Willy-nilly it became a faith. We had sold ourselves into its slavery, manacled ourselves together in its chain-gang, bowed ourselves to serve its holiness with all our good and ill content. The mentality of ordinary human slaves is terrible – they have lost the world – and we had surrendered, not body alone, but soul to the overmastering greed of victory. By our own act we were drained of morality, of volition, of responsibility, like dead leaves in the wind.

T.E. Lawrence, *Seven Pillars of Wisdom*

Bathed in the glow of the cosiness of my earlier life, I had always thought of myself as a person of unusual gentleness and a natural liking for other human beings. I now learned that I could hate intensely . . . and that I was capable of cruelty . . . Finally I was forced to think that my sophistication, easy sociability and worldly tolerance had been a form of carefully protected ignorance of life that had fooled myself.

Angus Wilson, *The Wild Garden*

Then a cold hard wind seems to blow through him. It is at once violent and peaceful, blowing hard away like chaff or dead leaves all the desire and the despair and the hopelessness and the tragic and vain imagining too.

William Faulkner, *Light in August*

Prologue

Retrospection

I HAVE a thing about hats.

At university in 1980, it was my black Rhodesian Army medics' beret. I stripped the badge off. I wore it backwards, puffed-up, golfer-style over my eyes – only now and then raked down across the right ear in the approved military manner. I was literally days out of my final National Service camp, and somehow not quite ready to let it go. The whole campus knew me by the beret.

Until an older Rhodesian – Zimbabwean – student said to me coldly, 'I wish you'd throw that bloody thing away, I've seen enough of them to last me a lifetime.'

I was abashed; he was right. That beret was like the memory you don't know where to place: the memory of a terror you are proud of having survived; the good memory that seems illegitimate somehow; the memory of hurts that have become essential to your being. A memory which, once displayed to the public, twists around in your hands like a live thing.

I wore the beret for another week out of defiance, then quietly replaced it with something more pacific.

The memories themselves changed. Twelve years later I was back on the same university campus, a lecturer now. I found myself talking to the father of a student of mine. She was utterly angelic but disappointingly unfocussed. Her father, himself a military man, bristled his moustache at me. He thought she should be sent to an Army training camp, to 'teach her some discipline'.

Like a bile in the throat, all-but-forgotten memories resurfaced: the tart smell of gun-oil, the abrasive textures of webbing heavy with death, the wet red caves of corporals' bellowing mouths.

Wounds.

I had a nightmare vision of steel-capped boots bludgeoning this winsome and beautiful soul into insensibility, or suicide. Worse, she appeared to agree with him.

'Don't you dare do anything like that,' I begged. 'The military is the most destructive, the most demonic system humans have ever invented. Don't.'

'You lived through it,' she pointed out. 'Was it all so bad?'

I had to admit, it hadn't been all bad. Maybe that was what the beret had been about. So what was this new and trenchant pacifism of mine?

It seemed a good point at which to revisit that most dramatic, most bizarre experience of my life. I dug out all the relics. There were a few dozen letters to my parents, who had stored them like heirlooms. There were some stories, vignettes really, attached to publishers' rejection slips. Even a few photographs of me, camouflaged, armed, lunging towards the camera, looking almost happy to be posturing that way. Most important, most solid, there was a collection of twenty stubby black diaries. They felt so familiar in the hand: their slightly yellowed newsprint texture, their scarlet canvas spines marked with ballpoint stripes like military ranks. Their faintly pollinated scent seemed not to have changed in all that time. The handwriting was recognisably mine, though it was tighter then, more constrained, and since then I'd modified my s's, closed those collapsing b's.

Rereading this record was unsettling. Most unsettling of all was an essay I'd roughed out sometime in 1979, which is to say after fifteen months of being subjected to the most demonic system humans have ever invented. The essay was entitled, 'For the Experience'. It begins:

> If a young lad were silly enough to ask me for advice, came up and asked me, Do you think I should go through Army? I would say, Yes. Without doubt, I would say.

The bulk of the essay is more ambivalent, even self-deceiving. I tried to balance the 'filthy and sordid and degrading' against the 'beautiful and funny and touching'. I wrote about how deprivation taught you appreciation of simple pleasures like 'a bed without rocks'. I wrote about how you learned to control 'the sheer primitive savage violence you never knew you had within you', and how, having outfaced death, you learned to love 'just the *fact* of Life with a capital L'.

Having said that, I thought that fighting for one's country was *not* intrinsically a 'wonderful thing'. And even more oddly: 'Given the choice, I would not have gone through with it, but now that I have I will never regret it, would do the same again.'

That could only have been written by a boy who had not yet confronted the real enormity of what he was doing, and the greater horror of his absolute lack of guilt.

But then guilt had never been allowed. Guilt implied caring, a conscience, and choice. Conscience was precisely what we had been systematically shut out of. Choice was like a garden filled with light and steaming plants, where growth happened, and new flowers were painfully born. 'Do it,' I wrote, 'go to war – just for the experience.'

I had to shake my head in disbelief. On another level, my motivation seemed perfectly clear. I had just spent fifteen months of my youth in a war, then in its most intense and futile phase: the period between Ian Smith's open surrender to 'majority rule' in 1978 and Robert Mugabe's taking over power in 1980. I was terrified that those months might turn out to be perfectly meaningless.

And rereading those self-cocooning pages, I realised that I was still afraid. I had tried to write it out of myself then, and failed. I still wanted to write it out, to write it into meaning.

But to what end?

Perhaps no one has put it better than a survivor of Auschwitz, the wonderful, tortured, ultimately suicidal poet, Primo Levi:

> I had returned from captivity three months before and was living badly. The things I had seen and suffered were burning inside me; I felt closer to the dead than the living, and felt guilty at being a man, because men had built Auschwitz, and Auschwitz had gulped down millions of human beings, and many of my friends, and a woman who was dear to my heart. It seemed to me that I would be purified if I told its story, and I felt like Coleridge's Ancient Mariner, who waylays on the street the wedding guests going to the feast, inflicting on them the story of his misfortune. I was writing concise and bloody poems, telling the story at break-neck speed, either by talking to people or by writing it down, so

much so that gradually a book was born: by writing I found peace for a while and felt myself become a man again, a person like everyone else, neither a martyr nor debased nor a saint: one of those people who form a family and look to the future rather than the past.

In what way exactly might writing make one feel more human? It has to be more than mere catharsis, a one-way leaching of the sea-salt of grief through 'rhyme's vexation', as the poet John Donne called it. It has to be more than mere self-justification. Self-justification can happen privately, as at a confessional, and doesn't need to be taken further. And it has to be more than just showmanship, though maybe that's a facet of all writing. Jean-Paul Sartre, the French existentialist, says:

> Each one has his reasons: for one, art is a flight; for another, a means of conquering. But one can flee into a hermitage, into madness, into death. One can conquer by arms. Why does it have to be writing, why does one have to manage one's escapes and conquests by writing? Because, behind the various aims of authors, there is a deeper and more immediate choice which is common to all of us.

That's it. A *deeper and more immediate choice*. In writing, I want, somehow, to reassert a freedom of choice which I feel I have been denied, or have not had the courage, or have been too blind, to exercise. I must choose to recall what happened, and I must choose to imagine the alternatives. Only then can I make any judgement about who I am, how I behave, and what I write. Only in this imagining can I gain and demonstrate the freedom which permits me to rebuild my humanity.

Writing will not be the end of it: the memories are reinforced, not exorcised. I do not believe I will be purified by it. No doubt I will continually have to remake, refurbish, re-judge, patch and bridge over the flaws in my own accounts of myself. And readers may not agree with my judgements – but that is beside the point. I have to present someone, a reader – any reader – with the opportunity to share in the freedom of judgement I exercise. I do not know if any writing can even in a small way, redeem the absolute silence which I have inflicted on others. So much is inevitably lost, dismembered, misre-membered: perhaps nothing is fully redeemable.

Can this writing be anything more than just another 'beret'? I'm not sure. But we have nothing to share but this common fallibility, and the knowledge that each of us harbours a rich and unique private world. Paradoxically, we have nothing to share but our privacy. I know that everything I say will be tainted with wondering if I have really left anything behind. Is it possible to grow out of oneself? Hasn't memory become impossibly disorientated among the tricky labyrinths of the imagination and self-justification? Is there a mirror which does not distort or a story which, even in its distortions, does not tell too much?

* * * * *

PART 1

Educating Snow White

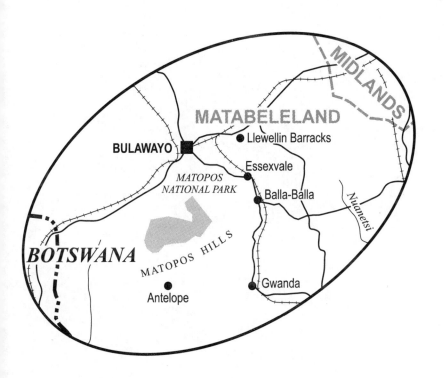

Chapter 1

The World is Elsewhere

MY FATHER'S bulky red fist lifts in salute for one last time above the yammering heads of my schoolmates and their desperate parents and sisters. He is not one for prolonged farewells, and I am glad. There is to be no room for sentiment in the man I have to become. There is a last-minute rush to the doors, a crescendo of girlish cries, a forest of flapping hands. The train tears away from its previous life, like muscle ripped slowly from bone. A war of feeling starts up in the middle of my chest.

That piratical fist represents all that is powerful about my father. It is at once supportive and daunting. It represents the philosophy of practical aggression he has tried to raise me in. In his native Ulster, in the merchant marine, in the Australian bush, in Rhodesia's Police Reserve, he has lived a lot on the rougher tiers of life. He is a self-made man. He has striven for years to drum into his dreamy, poetical son some of his engineer's pragmatism, his fighting thrust. As a kid I was taken to karate lessons, punched the air alongside enormous men, feeling silly and fragile, the soles of my young feet squeaking on the polished dojo floor. He taught me to box with a punchball tied into a sack and suspended from a branch: *C'mon, quicker, in and out, straight from the shoulder, too slow!*

I am entering my father's world, this moment when I step from platform to train in my home town, Umtali, on the morning of 3 January 1978, to go to war.

Unwillingly, I look back once more down the platform but of course he is lost behind the curve of the rails. All I see is a scrawny little brown dog being thrashed with sticks by three boys. Its yelps rise thinly through the hoarse champing of the diesel engine that hauls us helplessly away. Other boys – young men, my comrades – hanging through the windows beside me, laugh.

Feeling sick, I turn back into the compartment. My friends are talking weapons: I hear *seven-six-two, Magnum, hole the size of your head*. Of course, my father has taught me to shoot, too. Before the age of eleven I was firing the .22 rifle. The first time he took me out I couldn't hold the barrel out of the mud. And having been instructed not to point a gun at *anyone*, I pointed it at him – mimicking the shot, *phkheew!* – in a perfectly unpremeditated Oedipal spasm. He was knowing and gentle about it. Later it was our bolt-action .303 carbine: the dark wood of the stock felt weighty and dramatic after the slender .22; the word 'carbine' rang of the Wild West.

And finally the FN: professional, lean as a cheetah, the long butt hard to nestle into my shoulder because it was constructed for real men.

Many of the boys on the train can shoot; many are farmers' sons; the war has been with us for a long time. All of us from Umtali Boys' High have paid the necessary homage, in false but feeling prayers, to the old-boy casualties. Their names are listed in white on boards hanging in the school chapel, from Ronald Binks in '71 down to those familiar faces who left the school just last year and got the chop.

There are some here who have climbed aboard, prising away the fingers of their mothers, who will also not survive.

I realise, distantly, that I cannot be sure that I will survive.

For no obvious reason, the train stops for seven minutes. I write that down. I will deny all meaninglessness by writing things down. Nothing is to be forgotten. I have decided that this is to be The Great Adventure and a Formative Period. I will make, or invent, momentous literary capital out of the most banal of happenings.

Priggishly, I comment on the drunkenness that sweeps through the train in raucous waves: 'three hours on the rails, many already off the rails'. Potatohead lies on his back, snoring and ashen under stubble, his neck bent at an impossible angle. Beerbottles are hurled against passing poles, showering carriage windows with coppery shrapnel. Sunbundle sprays a passing carriage with frothing Coke just as the trains stop. A colour-sergeant in camouflage storms aboard: 'Don't you look so blerry innocent, you'll get your face smeared down your shirtfront, pipsqueak.' I giggle uncomfortably. Lanky Neil Downhill, friend of many years, dangles a cigarette from his wetted lips. I am disappointed in him. 'The Army will only intensify that,' I write with cynical foreknowledge.

So others piss it up; I judge. In our various ways, we struggle to enter our manhood.

2.10 P.M. Macheke. Picked up only one recruit.
2.30 Theydon. Never heard of it.
2.45 Tarasira. Never heard of that either. Near Peterhouse, by the trees.
3.00 Marandellas. Leave 3.25. Clouded over, rainy wind. Everybody has quietened. Rumour floating that we're being picked up by 2 Brigade in Salisbury, brought back to train. We'll see.
Bromley. Rain brief and stopped. Washed-out afterstorm sunlight on dark clouds. Stops at Ruwa etc.
5.05 SALISBURY.

So it goes on, painstaking, miniaturised. We transfer trains, wait, are released for an hour. I walk out into the streets alone. Orange lights flick on in the blue evening. I put on my new glasses. For nine years I've resisted wearing specs. I survived my short-sightedness by screwing up one eyeball with a finger, my father used to mock me about it, *See that flower on the wall? What wall, I don't see any wall.* Now I've figured out that if I can't see what's happening I am liable to get myself shot. It's almost a different world I enter now: buildings leap into focus, straight lines take on strange curves, the tarmac seems just half an inch further away than it used to. I float disconcertingly, paddle for a new balance.

Back at the station, I distance myself from the rumours that we will be met by General Walls, Commander-in-Chief, the 'Main Manna' himself. At 7.40, with no sign of Walls, we leave for Bulawayo. We have fallen almost into silence, wrapped in the tension of having so many strangers, all the Salisbury boys clamouring in the corridors, swamping our little Umtali contingent.

The night passes sleeplessly. I take refuge in silently composing and memorising a description of the 'rhythmical-awkward never-constant clack and rumble of the points; wheels or linkages silvery-musical click and squeal like trailing wire; growl and engine-surge on the uplines; sparks flying disconsolately past the window'.

I am the poet in the machine, unprotected and afraid.

* * *

5.50 A.M., 4 January. Heany Junction. An obscure meeting of rails in the bush north-east of Bulawayo, bearing a once household name. Captain Maurice Heany was one of those walrus-moustached pioneers and destroyers of Lobengula's Ndebele in 1893, a russet-headed Virginian, a forerunner of the American mercenaries and adventurers I will soon be meeting in our own Army. No doubt we are expected to emulate him. Heany had, wrote another rapacious hunterhero F.C. Selous, 'that dogged perseverance and untiring patience which has already won half the world for the Anglo-Saxon race'. It is the heritage of that race which, stumbling sleepily from our train, we are about to begin to fight for.

Or so we have always been told.

We disgorge from the train onto blue-grey railway gravel and grass, slump and mill through puddles and mud, spines twisted sideways with the weight of luggage. We heft our black tin trunks, painted with our six-digit Army numbers. I am 232154: already I remember it as clearly as my birthdate. Rumours have flourished on the train like fungus in a hothouse: *We have to run with our katundu from Heany to Llewellin, We don't get any hot water for the first week, If you oversleep and have to get picked up in Bullies they charge you with going AWOL, The first ambush drill is on the way there, I reckon that's bullshit, no one would . . . ja, but my brother said . . .*

Despite being summer, it is cold. I am being determinedly literary. I sit down for a moment and in the diary compare this frigid grey Matabeleland morning to Siegfried Sassoon's First World War dawn, 'Dirty white and chill with a hopeless rain'.

Knocked-about, gruff trucks and gloomy green buses arrive. Motley and muddled in our sundry clothing we load up. Already I'm feeling awkwardly, markedly 'civilian', inappropriately gaudy. Trucks bog down, are offloaded again, churn mud across jeans. A shanty latrine is run down in a clamour of corrugated iron. We do not have to run anywhere.

Llewellin Barracks. Not so grandly named, I somehow learn, after the first governor-general of the Federation. In a nervous confusion of barrack-rooms, iron huts, 1940s hangers left over from the place's airfield days, we begin the metamorphosis, the numbing separation from our younger lives.

Two days' movements gel into a miserable morass of rain and shouting. March here, march there. Hurry up and wait. My belly growls and aches with nervousness; I blame it on the humidity and heat, can't eat. We gather in this vast hanger or that. A cyclostyled 'Welcome' sheet I judge to be 'totally useless'. We utter Oaths – to Country, to God, to Corporal? – dentists assault our teeth, medics finger our balls and tell us to cough. Military kit replaces civvies, right down to razors and underpants. We curse our mothers for supplying us with 'everything you need', which we now have to lug from one mistaken barrack to the next. Rainsoaked, oversized battle-jackets abrade our thighs. At age eighteen, we sign our Last Wills and Testaments.

All this, I write to my parents, is 'incredibly boring'. I wish we were 'working our oats out'; the weather is 'depressing', I am 'dog-tired'. But I remain staunchly upbeat: 'Once fully into the swing we shall no doubt get along famously . . . I have not yet been rendered incapable of laughing.' I give them 'all my love'. After all, there is no one else in this grey place to give it to.

* * *

The more miserable I feel, the more I fool around. The remnants of our Umtali group hunch their shoulders in a corner of a teeming hanger, waiting for God only knows what. I take to imitating the officers passing by, their expressions, their strut. A man comes in from the rain in a dripping and swishing rain-cape. I do a flamenco dance. The man turns and sees me. He comes and thrusts his face close to mine, his breath smells of old gun-oil.

'You ponce, you *dog*! D'you think you're freakin' Greta Garble, or what? Whatever poncy pulp you're carrying in that skull you leave it behind, you unnerstand? You *forget* about the world out there, it's gone, it's somewhere else, *this* is your world, and it's *my* world, and you put one foot wrong you're *mine*, I'll have you shovelling my dung, you hear me?'

We retreat, shaken, to some tiered benches, look down on the rows of seated, shuffling rookies. Instructions boom from the mouths of lantern-jawed sergeants, blending and echoing until they become nonsense.

'Not a black face in sight, ay,' Bellicat remarks. 'Why the hell don't they call *them* up?'

'Just as it should be, mun, they'd just be underfoot.'

'Don't forget three-quarters of the Army is already black, chum,' Tall reminds us.

'Weird. What am I doing here? I should just bugger off to Spain and leave them to it.'

The man I mimicked has taken off his olive-green cape, his epaulettes bear the pips of a lieutenant. I watch him pacing up and down. I fear and hate him. His heavy face hangs in red folds, his eyes are unforgiving slivers. He flings enormous feet forward beneath a sagging paunch, florid hands hang loose as a gunslinger's. His poise is casual and dangerous. I hear his voice, snarling and lucidly enunciated; he is pushing the muzzle of his 9mm pistol into some poor innocent's ear, 'This thing will blow your freaking head off!'

I dub him Whorehound.

So I cling, desperate and futile, to fleeting contacts with friends and acquaintances, note their every move, our every separation. A sort of ambling, careless tornado redistributes, scatters, momentarily reunites us and, finally, without conscience, tears us apart. Farewells are repeated and repeated. Some of us volunteer for this or that unit: Signals, SAS, Selous Scouts. Others are dragooned: fine athletes for the sedentary Guard Force, morons for Intelligence. Mole-like Barrel, shifting from one small foot to another and hoping desperately to be a nothing, volunteers for Police, confident he'll be rejected for being too short, can become a nothing again. He is accepted. He disappears.

And me? I sign up to become an Officer.

* * *

'OSBies'. For the moment, we belong to the Officer Selection Board.

We are hived off from the others, rebarracked, supplied with numbered bibs, front and back, like racehorses. I am No.73. We watch a scratchy film on the Gwelo School of Infantry. This is where we will go, if selected. I judge the footage, with all the certainty of the completely ignorant, 'old and inaccurate'. We are given a lecture on ZANU/ZAPU's Order of Battle, our first insight into our enemy. It's an odd talk, contradictory. Our lecturers seem torn between unnerving us with the vision of an organised enemy to be reckoned with, and comforting us with the image of an ill-trained rabble ready to scuttle at the first shot. We feel privileged to receive a briefing on the national security situation. We have become the insiders, we are at the heart of the matter. I am interested to discover that there is an Operational Area named *Grapple*, another of those strong, resonant code-names someone has a talent for inventing – *Thrasher*, *Repulse*, *Tangent*. They make us feel stronger somehow – but what do they represent? A quiver of apprehension stirs in my belly.

Grapple is right in the middle of the country. We have already been overrun.

On the one hand, in these first few days, I am actively resentful at the lack of attention from the powers-that-be: no inspections, no exercise. I want to be driven, to feel myself grow. On the other hand, we are doing *intelligent* things: IQ tests ('two easy, one very difficult'), interviews, tactical problems. We have to write essays: 'Why I want to be an Officer'; 'Why I *should* be an Officer'. I wobble glumly between humility and hubris, unable to see myself in an honest light. But nothing in this exercise calls for honesty.

I have to deliver a lecture to my comrades. I decide to hector them on 'The Value of Learning from your Mistakes'. The lecture is loaded with enough self-importance to deter them from following me to anything more dangerous than a movie. Copying Hegel, I draw lessons from history on how no one learns from history: 'the countries of Africa are a case in point, each one suffering as they handed over to black rule, and if someone sneezes at the wrong moment it'll happen again in Rhodesia'. However – and this is my main point – 'If you're making no mistakes, it implies you know everything and have reached a state of perfection – and the way I see it, in the Army there's no such thing as a state of perfection. So mistakes must be accepted as not only inevitable but desirable.'

Possibly the lecture itself is *my* mistake. We head out into the rain to tackle a series of tactical obstacles. I start directing my section over a hurdle of walls and splintered planks. If you fall in the gap you'll be eaten by a croc.

The officer in charge yells at me through the misty air: 'What's the matter with you, are you a disaffected traffic cop, or what?'

My career as OSBie No.73 is brought abruptly to a halt.

* * *

'Laugh it off, never let it get you down,' I had exhorted my fellow-OSBies. I remember some veteran regular soldiers we met on the train, saying of Llewellin, 'You have to treat it as a joke.' But having humped my kit to yet another barrack, another constellation of unknown people and possibilities, I write home miserably:

> *Despite my determination to not care a damn, I am very disappointed. I could almost cry . . . of 174 entries for OSBies, about 60 eventually have gone to Gwelo . . . I have now been thrust into a totally different section of humanity, and a much lower one, I might add. Only last night we were discussing the nature of the universe; now I am among people who talk about nothing but the Army and are incapable of putting together a four-word sentence without three swear-words. I am still alienated from most of this scum . . .*

C Company, 9 Platoon. All the OSBie privileges – raincoats, leisure-time, separate eating-tables – have evaporated:

> *Almost before we're in we're out again and running, corporal screaming. Already we have to prepare for inspection tomorrow, and it's practically impossible to make wet boots shine. I am isolated, confused . . . My spirits are about as low as the cloud-level, which is floor-level. It's true that OSB probably knew what they're doing, and I would have been unhappy at Gwelo as well – I must just take it as it comes.*

Whorehound's face of flayed pork troubles my dreams.

Snobbery is my way of fending off my misery but I can't keep it up for long. I quickly find there are people I like here after all, and take a sly enjoyment in writing sketches of the characters I don't. I even take mildly to our sergeant and corporals. But I sense that isolation will always remain both my armour and my curse.

I fling myself into the activity. PT at 5.30 A.M.; pokey-drill with our rifles; marching drill in an echoing hanger where sergeant's and corporal's bellows merge with the bleats of a tribe of goats corralled at one end. 'Lunch,' whispers Neil Downhill. Lectures on grenades; films on hygiene; practice with stripping and assembling the heavy MAG machine-guns; furious late-night polishing for morning inspections. I absorb like a sponge anything that is scented with intellect. I grunt with satisfaction at good 'graze', fret at instances of disorganisation, lament the chunks torn from my knee when I slip on a run around the airfield. I feel the satisfaction of muscle hardening and refining itself. I chortle at the anal humour of 8 Platoon's motto, 'Semper in Excretis' – which they are: their loping, banshee-voiced corporal has them bunny-hopping round the barrack after supper until they vomit, running to the end of the road at two in the morning, carrying their twanging iron beds. We in 9 Platoon are lucky with corporals, we don't do that shit.

Nothing goes into the diary other than this minutiae: no sense of what is happening in the country, little sense of anyone's motivation for doing this stuff at all. Little sense of the aggression, the doubts. So much seems to be missing, as if subconsciously I am still writing for my mother.

Which is exactly as it is meant to be: the activity itself is the anaesthetic with which all subversive thought-patterns are dulled, and finally cut away.

* * *

'Yes, corporal.'
'I can't hear you.'
'*Yes, corporal!*'
'*I can't hear you!*'
'YES, CORPORAL!'
Why this insane shouting? Because it is not manly to mumble? Mostly because it is a sign of the corporal's power over you; there can

be no doubt among your hearers, even those on the next parade-ground, that your obedience is absolute.

Tall (who looks too big to need God, but is recently Born-again), replies mildly to the tempestuous upbraiding of five-foot-six Corporal Nottenuff:

'You don't have to swear at me, corporal.'

Nottenuff turns scarlet from beret-brim to collar. His blond mous-tache (as much a badge of rank as his solitary stripe) is as erect as a boar's mane. He stands on tiptoe to get as close as he can to Tall's flushed face. Closeness is an index of his fearlessness.

'Don't you fucking tell me what I need, you big *shit*! I don't care how fucking big you are, I'll break you in pieces, you're just a big arsehole around here, you hear me, you big fucking *cunt*! . . .'.

Tall stands and takes it – not only because he is a good Chris-tian, but because he too has a sense of the enormous weight of authority behind Nottenuff's pathetic moustache, the ready ma-chinery of coercion that waits to crush dissent. From the corners of our eyes we watch Tall's face shrink into itself.

Nottenuff turns away and winks at his fellow-corporal. He enjoys this; the madness is a sham. Why these gratuitous displays of au-thority, repeated a hundredfold, daily? Are they purposeful, calculated? Or just the whims of born bullies? Either way, we are being taught not only to give up reason, to submit without question; we are being taught to pass on the fury of our many defeats. Every order stings; every exchange is loaded with the language of insult and belittle-ment. We can feel the resentment banking up inside us like a dark fire.

In exchange we are given the minimalist pride of polished belt-brasses, of the unison of crashing boots, of the neatness of hospital-bed corners, of the act of obedience itself. Strange how quickly this pride takes hold of our lives; strange how quickly knowledge filters through on the best methods to bone a boot with spittle and a candle, to shape a black beret, to back the tin maltese-cross badge of the Rho-desia Regiment with a plastic disc cut from a deodorant top. The cultishness of these fragments of know-how makes our uniformity something more than mere fearful self-preservation. It is becoming a kind of professionalism, a bond.

But eventually the anger, the feeling of being chained down, has to be neutralised by being passed on to someone else. Another victim must be found. This is what the corporals are already doing. They are like parents who deal with their own hurts by projecting them onto their children. This is what we 'children' must also do.

Fortunately, the State has an enemy all lined up, awaiting our increasingly vicious attentions.

Despite the uniforms, the ferocity and shouting, the rules imposed on this unique world, individuality bulges like mercury into every available cranny. Friendships and conflicts are pressure-cooked. Red-headed, angular Crusty Bassoon and chunky, chainsmoking Irishman Fluecured are inseparable, even though they do nothing but fight. Graduates stand out: Ramrodd stalks about with supercilious ease; Michaelis carries his maturity with a quiet courtliness.

But the most powerful individuals are the criminal elements. They are no less clever. The tirelessly raffish, narrow-eyed Mekong is regarded as heroically self-promoting. Mekong survives by chutzpah, gross humour, and (usually) judicious aggression. Pipstring, by contrast, is a 23-year-old survivor-by-guile who has opted out of the greater evil of the South African Defence Force by volunteering in Rhodesia. Gangly, too quick to bare his teeth, he has a rodent's unflinching gaze, John Lennon glasses. Bony manicured hands flutter on jutty wrists. He is glib, persuasive, both scorned and envied for his sharp tongue. He has cultivated insiders in the barracks administration who feed him all the hottest rumours.

Pipstring and Mekong find they have common acquaintances among the seedy drug and sex dealers of Hillbrow, swap endless stories of illicit escapades the way other people exchange party jokes.

According to Pipstring, stocky insubordinate Bellicat and I are the only 'real' individuals in the barrack. I am flattered but wary. I hope my independence shows in my suspicion of him. To his face I can only weakly grin, turn back to polishing my brasses with water-paper.

So my education progresses.

Imagine the shock to my untutored soul when, shortly after a grainy, orange-hued film on sexually-transmitted diseases (it is of course assumed that all soldiers are uninhibitedly virile, indeed *ought* to be), Mekong himself comes up to me.

'Shit, I'm in a flat spin, mun, that fuckin' movie . . . I've had this thing on my prick for about a year now, I didn't know what it was, this sore just won't heal, what'd they call it . . . ?'

'A *chancre?*'

'Ja, shit, I don't believe it, I just dunno what to do, mun.'

'Well, you'd better go down to the hospital and get it checked out,' sagely.

'You reckon? Thing is, I might have given it to my chick, Christ! But I must have picked it up from this other chick I fucked, but she was only bloody fourteen! How the fuck can you be fourteen and already carry syph?'

I refrain from asking, What kind of fourteen-year-old would have made love to *you*, if she'd had a choice?

I still want to think of it as 'making love'.

Pipstring professes to be equally shocked when I confess to still being a virgin. He generously offers to conduct me through the dens of Jo'burg and initiate me into maturity. *That* is the real world, he says. He'll even pay, he says.

I wriggle, non-committal. That particular elsewhere world seems to me, thankfully, unreachable.

Henceforth, Pipstring refers to me as 'Snow White'.

* * * * *

Chapter 2

Divine Accident

O N THE train down to Llewellin, I noticed that the recently-converted Tall had stuck a Christian fish-symbol on his trunk. It reminded me of W.H. Auden's lines, which I had learned at school:

> Piso's a Christian, he worships a fish;
> There'd be no kissing if he had his wish.

'That's nonsense,' said Tall, 'I enjoy kissing, and anyway that's idolatry.'

Tall also had a sticker that proclaimed, 'Christ for Rhodesia.'

'*That*'s idolatry,' I said.

I was the chief of atheists at school. I and the chief of Jesus-freaks – The Jeek – loathed one another. We had a public debate once on the existence of God. I was too cocksure to prepare for it, and so was intellectually demolished – but the vote still went against The Jeek, because he was hopeless at rugby and had irritated everyone with his genuine purity. But The Jeek was still forgiving enough to invite me to stay over with his family on play-rehearsal nights: the war was too intense and unpredictable to allow us to drive the twenty kilometres home after dark. I grew to like him and to appreciate the generous ways of his people. But I didn't soften as much as Tall, for whose defection from scientific respectability The Jeek was largely responsible. Ever since Standard One, when I burst into desolate, infuriated tears when told to do homework for a Catholic scripture class, God has remained, for me, an unprepossessing and improbable phantom.

Now, in the Army, the compulsion to 'worship' in the approved manner reaches its most absurd. We have to march to church on

Sunday. The preacher's voice booms and wanes in the huge and shabby cinema which doubles for chapel. Rain-sodden rookies fall asleep. Things are temporarily enlivened by the sentimental efforts of an evangelistic quartet. I am so starved of music that even their ama- teurish guitar-notes and unblemished girls' voices reduce me to *frissons*.

'I can't believe we're still supposed to sit through this crap,' Pip- string hisses. 'Aren't we grown up?'

'God is on *our* side, remember?'

'So why doesn't he sort out the frigging *weather*?'

'And it's not as as if the missionaries aren't supporting the gooks out there, bloody World Council of Churches, have they got a differ- ent God, or what?'

'Bloody World Council of Wankers.'

Yet we have no choice but to cling to this moral force: the hypo- crisy is in the very marrow of our culture.

As we emerge from 'church' into the sagging air, Pipstring mimics the Prime Minister's Addresses to the Nation: 'And God bless you all.'

'Stuff God, it's my lifestyle, mun, it's the only civilised style in Africa, you can't even include the rock-spiders these days . . .'.

'Ol' Smithy's doing the best he can, mun, the whole world's against us, ay.'

'Ag, but what's the point of talking, the munts only understand force, we'll give them fuckin' force, God or no God.'

'Listen, stuff all that, my cousin was raped and cut to bits and left in a field to bleed to death,' growls Bellicat. 'That's the reason I'm here, and it's the only reason, and it's the only good reason.'

We fall silent. Almost all of us personally know people who have died, been murdered, brutally ambushed. Our conviction has be- come strong and crystalline, like the callous on a bone from which the ligament has been repeatedly torn.

My second compulsory attendance at 'church' is a rather differ- ent affair.

* * *

Sunday morning, 15 January. As a company, we head for the nine o'clock service, marching with ragged and awkward pretension as only raw rookies can. A gingery scrub-robin of a corporal from 7 Platoon makes us chant the time.

'Christ,' Aldoboyle mutters from the corner of his mouth, 'does he think we're kids?' We are 9 Platoon, we are better, our corporals don't make us *chant*. Rebelliousness shows itself in a certain apathy in the ranks.

'*You!* Fartface with three legs!' Me. 'Too *slow!*' Corporal Scrub'bin orders me to double around the squad as it marches. The men are moving down the left-hand side of the road. I am pounding clockwise. As I run around the front of them I am careful not to get trampled on.

The next sensation is of a vague but all-consuming thump, I glimpse my FN skidding along on its cocking-handle beneath the smoking tyre of a BMW Cheetah, a dull, paralysing pain locks my left leg, as if bolting it to the ground.

Scrub'bin squeaks out a 'Squad'alt'; the driver runs around the back of the car. It is my own platoon sergeant.

Wiry, in his late forties, a boxer's flattened nose on a face like a shoebox, close-set blue eyes, with a voice like a bronchial didgeridoo and an Afrikaans accent, he would look more at home on the back of a tractor. Ex-Rhodesian Light Infantry and Selous Scouts, an accident has left him with a pin in his leg and a dragging hobble, but he is said to be trying again for Scouts. To us rookies, this bespeaks a kind of grim but admirable madness.

Tractorback is a reasonable man. At the barracks hospital, he defuses his concern with crass jokes.

'You think *you're* in bad shape. I'm gonna have to fork out twenny bucks for a new headlamp! That's nearly a week's wages, Christ, my wife'll kill me. And you don't wanna see my wife when she's pissed off, let me tell you . . . Nah, just kidding, just kidding . . .'.

My own damage is bruising, torn ligaments round the left knee, and a broken bone in the left hand. With unwarranted optimism, I write home, 'I'm going to be out of action for some days.' My chief worry is missing out on going to the firing-range the next morning to try out the MAG for the first time.

Despite its upbeat tone, I don't send that letter to my parents for another four days. In the diary I am more subdued: I only despondently gloat, 'Fame at last!', as it becomes clear that the 'whole camp' knows about the prang by lunchtime. And 'everyone', springing to the defence of the underdog, is insisting I should 'charge' the sergeant, or the corporal, or both – sue the shit outa them. *They* are obsessed with charging *us* for every petty offence; revenge for the rookie would be sweet for all of us.

Within myself, lying in bed that night, my leg wincing under me, I feel a dark tide of nausea and despair chilling me, like the advance of an infection.

Only in hindsight will it become clear that the accident is the most important event of my military career.

* * *

My first escape from the confines of Llewellin is to Bulawayo Hospital to have the broken metacarpal set. On my back in the operating theatre, there suddenly smiles down at me the face of the anaesthetist Dr Oliver Ransford. Ransford is looking a little older and gaunter than the photograph on the dustjacket of his book *The Rulers of Rhodesia*, which I read with relish in my school years. In his introduction to that book, in lines which thrilled me then, but which will come to seem rather self-deceiving, both well-meaning and naïve, Ransford wrote that

> it is often conveniently forgotten that the record of [Rhodesia's] white settlers compares favourably with those of the colonists of America and Australia, and that they have made Rhodesia a tremendous asset to the Western cause in Africa . . . Even though they come from different stocks, all modern Rhodesians feel great pride in their achievements; all are intensely patriotic and resentful of external pressures. They know that their primary task is to find the rapport and the compassion which will allow them to share the country for the common good.

I open my mouth to thank Ransford for his stirring work, but the prick of the needle has come already, and his lined, jug-eared, gently snaggle-toothed face sways briefly and is gone.

* * *

I join the ranks of the 'lizards': the scum, the skivers, the ailing, the degenerate. We limp along behind the rest of the company, 'left, slither, left, slither!'. The number of lizards waxes and wanes depending on what PT is in store, what route-march. If there is a punishment-march, the lizards are blamed. If there is a threat to an upcoming weekend pass, it's the lizards at fault. And lizards, it is intimated, never get passes, ever.

I am fortunate that my injury is visible, my white cast gleaming against all the camouflage like a lighthouse on an inhospitable coast. I am also famous. 'Met any BMWs lately?' 'What happened to you, get bitten by a Cheetah?' and even, 'You the guy who was in the ambush?' Others have impressive but less obvious complaints – like Aldoboyle with his bass voice, swift wit, and disconcerting habit of flickering the whites of his eyes at you, as if he is about to pass out. Aldoboyle *does* regularly pass out, collapsing from heat exhaustion on the parade-ground, the acne-pitted skin of his face burned to a deep salmon. I feel lucky when I see the blisters weeping on his back. But with chuckling fortitude, and against all medical advice, he struggles back out to the range or the drill hanger, only to collapse with a sodden thump again as the sun rises.

I wonder what keeps Aldoboyle going. The mechanics of authority? Personal loss? Some notion of national duty, barely formed and therefore more difficult to question? Ransford's myth that white Rhodesians are the moral heroes of the Western world? I am not entirely sure what keeps *me* going, but I continue to drag my leg to lectures. Sidelined, I watch the guys screaming self-consciously as they bayonet hanging bags spilling with cow's guts. Corporal Banshee of 8 Platoon demonstrates, hurling himself with maniacal yells through the mud and the soggy air. The target quivers like a live thing. He comes back trailing his elbows, an insane laughter in pale blue eyes. As unarmed combat ensues, there is undisguised delight as Halberd, a livid, block-like Brit who claims to have been in Vietnam, rolls Banshee in the grey sludge. As often as not, we hate our own kind, the kind we are expected to become. I am repelled, but also keenly feel my weakness in this gymnasium of aggression and strength.

The technical aspects interest me more than all this posturing idiocy: my first diary notebook ends, and the second begins, with notes and diagrams of types of grenades. So long as these technicalities remain on the page, untainted by political dogmas or actual blood, they somehow seem clean and warranted. It satisfies the fascination with the paraphernalia of warfare I have shared with my father from early boyhood. Even the undiscriminating lethality of enemy booby-traps, as explained one day by the garoupa-faced Sergeant Benderson, has this conscience-free attraction. Benderson has what looks like a bullet-wound on the wrist which he ostentatiously tickles, a depression into which the hair curls as if into a plughole. His flat grey eyes betray nothing as he relates:

'The gooks here are too stupid to try anything like this, but this was a Vietcong trick. The women in Saigon would fit razor-blades crosswise in a tube, which they'd shove up their cunts. When the Yank troopie dives in there for a good time, *zik!* Four times the action.'

And he carefully draws a diagram of this blood-curdling device on the chalkboard. Just so's we know.

This ambivalent sexuality runs through everything. Comments filter back from the massive movie-house about Whorehound's two blonde daughters, who sell snacks from a small back kiosk: 'Fucking sluts, wouldn't mind getting into those cheap pants.' 'Are you penga, they'll give you syph, man. Mushi melons though, ay?' There is that universal ditty we have to chant: 'This is my rifle [whack the plastic stock], this is my gun [clutch the genitals]'. Some 'sexual perversion' results in female terms like 'puss', 'cunt' and 'bitch' being liberally applied to males. And why is everyone always denigrating my mother? – 'Your mother screws goffles'; 'Your mother carries an AK'; or just 'Your *mother!*'

As a *bona fide* lizard, I miss drill and PT, route-marches, runs. I read a lot of novels, the *Reader's Digest*, and the *Illustrated Life Rhodesia*, a colonial rag which, I suspect, is the first to reintroduce the country's conservative readership to the naked nipple. I also read Heinz Guderian's *Panzer Leader*. Much of this hefty book is clotted with the numbing detail of an obsessive commander's battles:

I radioed Liebenstein to instruct XXIX Panzer Corps that SS-*Das Reich* be sent south to the River Udai, between Kustory and Perevolochinoie, and thence be directed on Ssrebnoie-

Bereskova in conjunction with the panzer Division. 10th (Motorized) Infantry Division was to advance on Glinsk . . .

And so on. Basil Liddell-Hart, another military writer I admire, explains in his foreword to the book:

> As a practical necessity a commander in the field often has to take action without reflection, and, even when he has the time for it, a habit of reflection on the remote consequences of the action ordered would tend to induce paralysis . . . It is easy to condemn Guderian's attitude as evidence of 'unrepentant militarism' – but wiser to recognize that his basic assumptions were a necessity of military service.

My diary, I begin to realise, is becoming another example of this syndrome. It details action without reflection; emotions are reduced to clichés and exclamation marks. The style is a combination of naïvety, haste, and boredom. In my crippled state, I have little else to say. I disconsolately sweep the barrack-room single-handed; I get landed with lackey-work like painting window-frames, moving chairs, helping the bristly Corporal Burgomeister clean out the Company Quartermaster's. Carefully I record that Burgomeister generously distributes to his helpers outdated girlie calendars and the answer-sheet to a passé map-reading test; that I pick up a pinless beret-badge for 'a souvenir', as if I am already thinking of all this as something to be merely travelled through and remembered.

I speculate obsessively about what is going to happen to this lizard who is rapidly falling behind in the training. Since I will not be allowed to go home, will I be 'back-phased', that is restart training with the second intake of rookies arriving in February? Will I be prevented from becoming an instructor, which I am thinking about as a way in to the teaching career I have already mapped out for myself? I grapple with rumours:

> *Somebody said Cpl Hamerkop said the Army didn't want instructors any more. Aldoboyle astutely reckoned this was political in origin, and that we wouldn't be in the Army much longer, or rather there wouldn't BE an Army much longer.*

As with T.E. Lawrence in the Arabian desert, my stress shows up in an outbreak of boils, hot volcanoes of pus and unpredictability. The only regular thing in my life is physiotherapy at 8.30 every morning. The fulsome and gypsy-like Mrs Bracefield caresses my glycerined knee with ultrasound. A casually vicious Corporal van Nouzens grinds the ligaments into new life with a bony thumb and a wolf-like grin. Finally, after a few weeks, I start loading my webbing with bricks and jumping over and over from the five-foot high bed of an abandoned trailer.

Although, from individuals to nations, what seems to make us who we are is the quality of our woundedness, I am beginning to learn from this that the real pride lies in the healing.

Over the weeks, my leg mends well, the hand poorly. An irritable specialist finally cuts away the reeking, fraying cast. The bone hasn't set at all. There is a mumble about an op, a wire pin. Then he sends me off to 'see what happens'. After that the only treatment I get is a couple of wax baths, which do little more than scald the skin. In time, the oblique fracture knits, but I will always have a knuckle depressed by a quarter-inch and a callous on the bone the size of a macadamia nut.

Not much to be proud of, if I were into being proud of war-wounds. Not much, compared to the scrawny, cheerful, mock-aggressive black soldier also in physio, shot through both legs, gaily and doggedly disproving the prognosis that he'll never walk again. We enjoy playful wrestles together, he sneaks in punches and reels away on his awkward legs, laughing.

Nothing, compared to what many of my friends will suffer.

In fact, the only 'war-wound' of my entire career to which I can concede any long-term discomfort is inflicted while I am on a weekend pass. And is perfectly invisible.

Weekend passes come quite thick and fast, despite all rumours to the contrary, adding weight to my vicarious conviction that 'the Army isn't what it used to be'. Once, I make it home to the high hills of the Vumba, jostling on trains and hitching with wondrous efficiency. In my parents' presence, I do not know where to place my hands, how to compose my face. I don't know how to dispense my new knowledge, or soothe their worries about my injuries. I am torn between discomforts. My father, ever concerned about my survival, carts me out to the firing-range at Gimbokkie, where I blaze away at a cardboard box with my Army FN. Driving home, I am explaining something to him, and he says, 'Why are you shouting?'

I realise that I cannot hear the sound of my own voice through the ringing in my ears.

This tinnitus diminishes after a few hours, but will never leave me entirely. On quiet nights it is there to remind me of a certain frailty, ineradicable as a memory – a thin, persistent, unvarying scream out of nowhere.

* * *

1 February. *Lunch brings unwelcome news – I, along with Aldoboyle, Shambolas and others, have been kicked down the slope into B Company. My immediate reaction is precisely the same as that I experienced when I failed OSBies – disappointment, trauma of dislocation, again.*

The C Company 'scum' of only three weeks ago has been transformed into 'this fine bunch'. C Company kit is handed in; I regret being divorced from my workable FN, No.240, with its tarmac-gouged cocking-handle. But I am not even to join the troopies of the line: I am to help out as general factotum at the Company offices. I will sleep in a small, frequently empty barrack in the NCO lines, a room a quarter-inch deep in dust, beds leaning against the wall like skeletons in an ossuary.

I am glad for the relative privacy, but there's also a real loneliness, seeping through like a mould.

Next morning I report to the B Company office, tapping tentatively at the door. A bellow invites me in. I almost turn and bolt. Lieutenant Whorehound has some miscreant rookie down on his knees with that black 9mm pistol stuck in one ear and the florid, froglike face snarling in the other. He looks up at me appraisingly with his quartz eyes glistening between the chapped lids.

'What's the matter, soldier, lost your mother? Stand up straight in my office, you one-armed bandit!' So this is Whorehound's territory. I curse the stupid, uncaring machinery of God or the cosmos or whatever the hell it is that governs my life, for landing me here – of all the appalling places.

'Well, I don't know, sweep the blasted floor for all I care.' And off he stalks, thrusting out his belly, flinging his big feet forward as if kicking kittens, smirking with a kind of phlegmatic exasperation, shaking his head at everybody else's stupidity, tugging the pistol from its olive holster and pointing it at his own head and pulling the trigger on the empty chamber and putting it back and shambling on without changing his pace or his disdainfully suffering expression.

While waiting for him to find me something more to do, I am seconded back to C Company to help repaint their buildings, the older corrugated-iron and plywood types. Tractorback is there: 'Aren't you the fucker who smashed my headlamp?' In vest and shorts he looks older, frail. His spine curves around his erect and rigid will, like a snake around the caduceus. Long scars on his legs where the metal pins went in. I cannot imagine him getting back into Scouts; then I look at the mica chips of his eyes and imagine he could.

For the next six weeks I am nervously engaged in clerk's work, surrounded by NCOs and officers, bungling my salutes, at the beck-and-call of all of them. Whorehound calls me 'The Arm'. Most other people he calls 'snot-gobblers'. He snarls, sighs, jokes, acts almost fatherly. I don't know if I can trust him. I trust no one, keep my head down. My mind begins to feel clammy with dust and yellowing news-print, filing-cabinets, lists and lists of names which riddle my dreams.

Now it's lunchtime and I have time to consider, I'm bloody unhappy – again . . . Now I want out of Llewellin. But I mustn't brood – lump it, boy.

I hatch plans to escape, I will do anything to get out of here. I am not learning to become a soldier or a national asset: I am learning to be selfish and manipulative. I develop an obsession with levering myself into the Rhodesian Intelligence Corps (RIC). I haven't a clue what they do, the name is attraction enough for me. Aldoboyle has already chiselled his way into RIC, and now adds his considerable cunning to mine. I plague Whorehound, the company commander, sundry faceless people over the office phone. The weeks pass with plenty promised and nothing delivered.

Whorehound begins to make noises about keeping me on as clerk at Llewellin for the rest of my National Service. My throat fills with a nauseous hopelessness. I feel like the characters in Beckett's play *Waiting for Godot*, still fresh in my mind from school:

ESTRAGON: I'm going.
   He does not move.

* * *

I am slowly inuring myself to my temporary exile in NCO Barrack 31. In the half-dark I write poems of longing to unavailable girls. One of the elusive corporals has turned out to be the gingery Burgomeister from the Quartermaster. His moustache bristles horizontally at me at first – 'What the fuck are *you* doing in *my* barrack?' But possession is nine-tenths of comfort, and he is only in about once a week. Other corporals occasionally appear, switching lights on in the middle of the night, banging their way to bed. It is lonely, alienating, and spartan. I have become part of the grey machinery that keeps a war going, that its spurious glamour hides. I am buried in the Underworld.

And like Dante in the circles of the Inferno, I still note every glancing contact with recognisable souls: C Company friends being dumped into B Company, B Company troopies finding niches in the specialist units, old cronies being RTU'd (Returned To Unit), disheartened after failing the officer's course at Gwelo ('You couldn't lead ants down a hole in the ground').

The situation is not improved by the arrival of Misflitt.

Misflitt is one of those C-Cat (= medically unredeemable), apparently hopeless characters who occasionally get washed up on the Army's intolerant margins, doomed to gasp and flounder until thankfully ejected back into the kinder civilian sea. I cushion myself against his irritating, sucker-like presence first by trying to reform him and then, failing that, by turning him into Literary Material:

Mursil M Misflitt is the most pusillanimous and pathetic character I have ever met – and one meets all types in the Army. He is a lesson in decision in his very indecisiveness. I have heard all sorts of stories of how he acted before I actually met him. How he slept in full uniform. How he never polished his brasses. How he was forever on Sick Parade. How he got beaten up badly enough to develop a hernia that put him in hospital for two weeks and more. He ended up being back-phased from 160 to 161, and in the interim was placed in a position of clerical assistant alongside myself. I lived with this pathetic individual for twelve days, by which time, sorry for him though I felt, I was glad to see him go. Mursil is a slender boy with baby-curly blond hair to which he pays much attention – indeed he is femininely fastidious in all such matters, taking up to twenty minutes to get fully dressed. I wonder, however, how much this is due to fear. He is forever adjusting his beret with his thin, stuttering hands, forever making sure his trouser-legs are tucked into his boot-tops – not unusual in the Army, of course, especially when working all day with officers, but in Mursil's case to an inordinate degree. He lives on his nerves now, I think. His whole demeanour is nervous. His flat-dark eyes never rise to meet yours; his thin lips are always moving, accentuating the lines at the corners . . .

And so on. He cuts a sad figure and I patronise him terribly, trying to grind away my own timidity in the mortar of a desperate pragmatism.

* * *

10 March. At last, the break. Whorehound mutters out of the side of his loose mouth, 'I shouldn't be doing this, but how would you like to be a tracker?' I gape. Whorehound suddenly seems almost human, he actually recognises what I so desperately need. A National Parks unit will take on the training of half a dozen trackers. There is a swift interview. I am accepted. The Divine Accident has finally borne its strange fruit. If there were a God, I would give thanks. I write home:

I am now a Sparrow. No, I'm not, I'm a prospective Sparrow. Do you know what a Sparrow is? You don't? Well, I'll tell you. A Sparrow is a bird. But I am not a bird, or even a prospective bird. A Sparrow is also a National Parks tracker. Your astute and calculating brains will at this stage, before you reach the end of this paragraph of exuberant balderdash, deduce that I am a Prospective National Parks Tracker. End of paragraph.

I brush aside the worrisome aspects of this new job with gross bravado:

*It will be tough, much in the nature of Selous Scouts, and the job
which follows dangerous. Work will be entirely military, mostly recce,
and contact with the enemy probable. But I am determined to go
through with it, on the principle that a) anything's worth a try; b)
anything different is good experience; and c) anything's better than
being a clerk.*

I do not tell National Parks that I have scarcely mastered the
About-Turn.

* * * * *

Chapter 3

Birth of a Sparrow

I REJOIN training with relish, the harder the better: sheer activity is one antidote to meaninglessness. Muscle. Pain. The other is writing about it.

14 March (Tues). *A good day: starts off with PT at 5.30 – dark & overcast, good weather for a 3 mile run, though I'm horrified that we have to run in boots and denims. In the event we just trot around Married Quarters and then come back to root shirkers out of the barrack-rooms – and a good number of them, too! The boxers – boxing competitions are in full swing, so to speak – including Tall and Small, have been having their own workout – and they'll be getting quite a rev in the future, too. Even after this relatively light run, however, my legs are stiff, though I kept up well enough for the distance. Then to a healthy breakfast.*

The morning is devoted to another episode of the Whorehound Show, this time on Battle Procedure & Battlecraft, and the rest – most of it – to Skirmishing. A lecture by Sterek, followed by a demo involving blanks, smoke-grenades & thunderflashes. Then we try it ourselves – dirty work and quite tiring, though I shape up as well as any of them. A lot of kit lost out of webbing in the process. Finish this at 12.30, & cross to the gym for PT & Forward Roll with Rifle – from which I desisted after a while since my hand, already hurting after skirmishing, is not standing up too well . . .

A very hearty lunch: afternoon spent on lectures on rifle drills and on Ground & Cover by Motherson. Rather dry method of lecturing he has, very formal. His method of waking people up is to throw the firebucket of water over them. Actually finish early, and we're all look-

ing forward to a relaxed evening when in comes Sergeant McGinnagin and informs us we're on Fire Force for the night . . .

15 March (Wed). *Tough morning – no PT in the morning before breakfast! I decide to go to Sick Parade, partly because my hand is genuinely bugging me, partly to avoid RSM's drill parade. On arriving at the Hospital, I am immediately sent back because I don't have my kitbag. If I were dying on my feet it wouldn't matter, I must have the kitbag. I go and don't come back. I wait in the barrack-room until it becomes impossible to go to drill, writing a letter, then going down to the lecture-room. An hour of picking up cigarette-stubs, a lecture on Rifle Lore – firing, misfire drills – then PT – Leopard Crawl with Load, a 30-lb pipe filled with concrete. I kept up not too badly . . . Spent the rest of the day wet.*

Lunch, afternoon in lectures – Battle Formations, Silent Signals, Map Reading. Loooong sleeping tonight.

16 March (Thurs). *Not a day to look forward to, with 3 sessions of PT in the morning and skirmishing all afternoon. But the morning 3-mile run turns out to be nearer a quarter-mile, swimming we delayed away and did circuits instead . . .*

Lecture by Velosio on Radio Procedure – old hat after Agric-Alert – and by Sterek on tanks in general, including what the other sides have – T34s and T54/55s, as well as a couple of French makes. Didn't really teach me much . . .

So the details accumulate to build up one kind of a picture: laboured, amoral, even seduced by the training's approximation to an education, the revelling in physique shot through with spasms of apathy. Perhaps a year later, having changed my views somewhat, I will summarise this part of it all very differently:

Now the new soldiers hone their boots to a moon sheen, flesh their brasses with reflections, tender with breath and brush. Breech-blocks slide smooth as razors on cheeks. Crisp on empty chambers the triggers click. Stand by your beds. You slam to attention. The weasel-lean corporals sidle down the lines, all aligned, buttons and blankets and rifles and eyes. He comes to you, your eyes flicker, he thrusts his face down to yours, so close you can see the bruised red of his throat, screams moistly, Don't look at me, I don't love you.

No one loves here, not here among the tattered barracks where the ratchet marching saws perpetually across your mind. The rain is sifting down on a raw wind. You lie on your belly with your face in a brown puddle. Up. Down. Up. Down. Your triceps have lost their elasticity, wooden pain. Up. Down. Forty-nine. Down. Fifty. Not good enough, you. Fifty. Fifty. We'll stay on fifty until you all do it properly. Fifty. Someone is whimpering. Hate him, that one in the blue tracksuit, hate all the instructors, the officers, the RPs, the cooks, the uncaring medics. That's all right, that's what they're here for, that's what they expect. They preach hatred.

* * *

I have moved back into barracks with a mixture of relief and trepidation, choosing the half of 5 Platoon which I deem (as usual) 'the least worst of a bad lot'. I begin to make the tentative friendships that arise simply out of being closest. In the next bed there is Meretrich: well-built, shambling, flickering his pale lashes as he clamours for attention; he bubbles with dirty jokes, is as invasive of my privacy as a horse, has a naturally sleepy expression that perpetually gets him into trouble. Meretrich has also been accepted for the tracking course. Like it or not, I will have to get used to him. Almost as noisy but more amenable is Jorrock, small and stocky with a square, good-looking face, pitted cheeks and soft brown eyes and crows'-feet when he smiles. He is quick-witted, impish, and welcomes me by stealing my socks and tying them round the lightbulbs, where great reeking holes get burned in them. On the other side of me is tall Lumbis, strangely dark, with a gaunt face and a cynical, aristocratic twist to his upper lip; the large movements of his bovine jaw, a pushing-out of the lips, makes his speech slangy and exaggerated, effeminate as the way his wrists swing loose as he walks. He likes to know he's being watched or heard. I suspect insecurities, find him unthreatening. His favourite expression is, 'Oooh, you *bitch!*'

It does not even occur to me that Lumbis is gay.

And there is coppery Brinjal, slope-shouldered, livid with freckles, pedantic in speech, and in all ways scrupulous. A lugubrious expression hangs like an old coat around an enormous nose. I feel an unaccountable affection for sad Brinjal.

We begin to spend more time together, contriving to sit next to one another at meals, march alongside one another, talk. I begin to seek out that warming thread of companionship, the way I stretch for glimpses of a sunset between the unlovely barrack-room walls.

He's the son of married doctors, I learn. When he gets letters from them he sits on his bed with his boots planted flat, reads them quickly, and tears them up into long strips.

'Why do you *do* that?'

'They're so – sappy,' he says.

'We could do with more sappy in this dump,' I offer, gesturing at the bare-chested, barbed, raucous brawl going on around us. 'Parents are meant to be sappy.'

'Stuff that,' says Brinjal nasally, his accent so absurdly refined it reduces the curse to whimsy. 'It's like – like they're always standing there holding hands, in front of some stupid chapel or other. Grinning. They're so *perfect*, they're revolting.' And he tears the envelope into strips, too, but with such elaborate care it's as if he wants to make destruction itself a work of art. 'I'm never going to become bloody do-gooder doctors like them, that's for sure. I'm so glad for this Army thing, I tell you, I can do what I jolly well like, it's fantastic.' He looks around him with an expression of the profoundest misery.

I don't laugh at Brinjal, this would-be rebel who is possibly the most timid and conservative conformist I have ever met. His assiduous melancholy fascinates me. I write about him secretly. I probe.

Eventually it comes out, like the core of a boil.

'How old are your parents?'

'They're 65 or so. Crocks.'

'Really? And brothers or –'

'My sister's 22 years older than me. I hardly know her. I'm a kind of an only child really.'

'I *am* an only child,' I tell him.

Slowly, as if the words are too heavy for his tongue, he says, 'I bet you were *wanted*, though.'

That's it, I decide, that is the key. I like discovering keys. Knowing the key to a person is a special and secretive kind of bond.

Brinjal adds, with a strange twist to his over-sensitive lip, 'It makes me feel, well – like shit.' It is the one and only time I ever hear Brinjal use such a word.

I try to chaff him out of it, 'O yeah, right, you're such an evil, nasty brute, Brinje!'

Wordlessly, he goes back to polishing his boots, making me feel redundant and cruel, since in some impervious part of his being he evidently believes that. He polishes and polishes, so devoted to getting it all just right it hurts and exasperates – exasperates especially because I see reflected in his every sad, sedulous act the cowardice I suspect in myself.

* * *

I take especial note of the instructors' lecturing styles. Since I am thinking of becoming a teacher myself, I must learn from this, too. Whorehound is hilarious but incoherent, illustrating how *not* to do everything with anecdotes about the hypothetical, slap-happy, Hollywood-American troopie, 'jolling along, steel helmet, straps hanging down'. Our new Company Sergeant Major, Bristleton-Squalshe, bandy-legged, orange walrus moustache, and a voice like a strangled donkey, likes the sound of his own lecturing too much. He is appalled by our standards of fitness and discipline and I glumly predict that he will be 'sticking his bristles into everything'. Sterek, his lean and peppery face hewn into permanent expressionlessness, provokes enough interest to write home:

> A very accomplished man, this instructor . . . He is (or was) a) Rhodesia's national karate coach (he's offered to try and get us to see the International Championships in Bulawayo when they come round); b) a one-time mercenary in the Congo (1965); c) among the four top anti-tank men in the country, along with Sergeant Major Motherson; d) a holder of three pilot's papers (or something) in commercial aviation and a private pilot of 180 hours experience; e) chairman of a local parachuting and free-fall club. Among other things. All this discovered during a skirmishing lesson during which half-an-hour was spent skirmishing and an hour-and-a-half talking to Sterek.

For the moment, he is our hero. He promises us a parachute course.

I sign up immediately. It never transpires, perhaps was never meant to. Heroes, it seems, are going to be hard to come by. Even harder to become one.

* * *

On 3 March, at 10.20 A.M., Ian Smith, Abel Muzorewa, and Chief Chirau sign the Salisbury Agreement. This is a straw-clutching and immediately maligned 'Internal Settlement', which accepts one-man-one-vote and essentially signs away everything 'we' believe we are fighting for.

My diary entry for that morning rivals the complacency of Louis XIV's the day the Bastille was stormed ('*Rien*'). I write: 'The office proves about as dull as usual.'

But two weeks after the event, in the middle of all the ponderous accumulation of detail, like a glimmering promontory of intelligence on a low-browed shore, a political comment pops up in the diary. I muse:

> *I don't see the settlement affecting my call-up period, but will probably make it more dangerous. Certainly here the instructors are all-expectant of a full-scale war (hence the tank-training). With the Patriotic Front fully allied to the governments of Zambia and Mozambique, all three being Commie or going that way (Kaunda), an international war may well replace the nationalist one, which will probably peter out. So let's go tracking across the border!*

There's more of this false bravado a week later:

> *22 March. Transitional Government formed today. It will, at this stage, make no difference to my willingness to fight. A lot of guys are ratty about serving a black government, but in the last resort they'll fight because they're told to. Personally, I'm fighting for a standard of life; if the government starts wrecking those standards, I'll fight the government instead. Or go to Spain. Or something.*

A couple of days later, I manage a little more scepticism:

Smith says he believes the Marxist threat has been destroyed by the internal settlement. I don't believe it: if anything, that is all that is left once the bulk of the nationalist complaint has been removed. It is true that the Marxist forces have taken advantage of black nationalism in its customary fashion, and that their situation will now deteriorate, but it is also true that not the whole of black nationalism has been accounted for by the internal settlement; no matter what anyone says, Joshua Nkomo, if not Robert Mugabe, still holds a lot of sway, particularly in Matabeleland . . . A strong likelihood then is that a disgruntled Nkomo will go over to Marxism even more strongly than now, and combine with national Marxist forces like those of Mugabe and Mozambique and perhaps Zambia. The Rhodesian conflict will then become a case of Marxist-capitalist, east-West conflict pure & simple . . .

Most of this is hopelessly inaccurate and naïve, drawn from the pages of the *Bulawayo Chronicle* and over-exuberant bar-talk.

'I don't think we have to worry about Mugabe, fuckin' Commie, no one believes in him, mun.'

'Jeez, I dunno, hey, I scheme he's the main oke.'

'So we'll just take him out as soon as he pops his scabby head up.'

'Long, bazooka the shit. *And* Nkomo . . .'.

'I can't believe anyone still believes that Communist garbage, hey . . .'.

'It's like a fucking virus, you know, they can't help it, it affects anyone with less than three braincells . . .'.

'Nah, Bob or no Bob, we whiteys are stuffed, ay, we won't survive in Africa, look at the whole continent, man . . .'.

'It's different here, though . . .'.

'Yeah, buggered if I'm just gonna let them run us outa here, Jesus, I'm gonna take over my old man's farm, no matter what.'

No one seems to think that in fact white supremacist rule in Rhodesia has been on the skids for a good while, from at least the 1976 Geneva Conference, if not before.

But there is little time for political commentary. I am much too deeply buried in the thick of smaller things.

* * *

We are already going 'operational' in a minor and half-arsed way. At first we are assigned to patrol around the barracks at night. We are grandiosely termed 'Fire Force'. A buzzer goes, we lurch out of bed and into boots and scarves, Duty Sergeant McGinnagin – barrel-like, hirsute, dark as a Portuguese, aggressive and crafty – gives an unintelligible Scots growl between snores and leaves us to it. We ramble for half-an-hour around Married Quarters in a clapped-out truck and (if it doesn't break down) squirm sleepily back into bed.

More seriously, in late March – the Easter weekend – B Company is assigned to guard white holidaymakers in the Matopos National Park. It is an extensive and chaotic enterprise.

We are impressively briefed by a policeman who attempts to give us some idea of the nature of 'the blacks' in the area (some 18 000 in 600 square miles). He takes us through tribal, religious and historical perspectives, as well as practical hints in 'the identification of blacks' (whatever that means). Whorehound reports (and I carefully write down) that 30 'terrs' in civvy clothing are on a recruiting campaign, 'especially around places of religious significance, connected with the woman Nahanda (?) who instigated the Matabele Revolts of 1896'.

I am too ignorant even to get Nehanda's name right. Most of us still believe that all forms of 'native unrest' arise from some inconvenient and whimsical superstition. Despite the deficiencies of our colonial education, I find myself, as I listen to Whorehound's snarling voice, suspecting that this is a hoary imperial delusion. A memory stirs of that famous photograph of Nehanda and the medium Kaguvi, before their execution in 1898, looking dusty, frightened and beaten. She will become the most potent symbol of resistance to white rule. The story of her final enraged yelling and kicking on the scaffold of Salisbury Jail will be etched into the cultural memory of just about every modern Zimbabwean.

Into Nehanda's hills – the Matopos – (which in fact they aren't, Nehanda never came near the Matopos) Whorehound now leads his disorganised tribe.

Trucks and half-baked drivers are raked up at the last moment, and an openbacked, doorless Land-Rover for Whorehound. I ride shotgun with him, now his trusted shadow. We take along a gunner who straps on black perspex goggles and mask and mans a tripod-mounted MAG, looking like a vigilante out of George Orwell's *1984*.

Whorehound drives like a maniac; we barely have time to return people's patriotic waves as we rattle through Bulawayo's generous streets.

And then we are in the open. No sallow barrack walls, no shouting or gunfire – instead an engulfing silence wide as the sky, acacia trees, widowbirds dragging their extravagant tails across the gold fields. I realise how desperately I have longed for beauty, for variety, for the natural. As we whine through the Game Park, I am moved almost to tears by the curves of sables' necks and scimitar horns, nodding above swathes of yellow grass. The massive domes of Matopos rock overwhelm my starved senses. Everything is grandly wet, streams silver with quick gravity. My very skin exults.

Meanwhile, drivers are shitting themselves, easing their trucks along the narrow and flooded Maleme Dam wall. At the dam base, Bristleton-Squalshe is arguing with the chief ranger, who is gung-ho to lead the whole operation himself. So is the local cop; he has already forged ahead in making his own arrangements. 'The *dogs*,' snarls Whorehound, whips us up to the tourist chalets which are to be our base. Dumped in a sudden hollow of quiet, we amuse ourselves helping to erect a tent for the Pronto, the radio operator. Sterek is organising foot patrols from the Hotel. A lone signaller is discovered wandering, blissfully unarmed, along the road somewhere. 'You're a fucking lunatic,' yowls Whorehound; we have to take him back to the nearest road-block, manned by middle-aged Police Reserve 'Specials'.

'Specially old and not specially good,' Whorehound smirks.

I am fascinated by the primaeval, tumbled, balancing rocks of the Matopos, streaked with wholesome colour, clotted with impenetrable bush – and appalled by this terrain's suitability for the insurgents, and by our own vulnerability to ambush in the yellow-green vleis.

It occurs to me sharply that I could get killed in this operation. And I don't even have any dog-tags to identify me. We only get issued those when we are *fully* qualified to be killed.

In the meantime, it is Whorehound's desperate driving I have to be most concerned about. We start out again at dusk, the moon up, hands going rigid in the night chill. As we whine like a dispirited banshee between the hills Whorehound flashes a handheld torch around the bushes, a demented Cyclops. We skid to a halt to 'interrogate' two Africans. We don't much like the one with shabby, knotty hair. His name is Ndhlovu, a Sikalanga name, which Whorehound regards as particularly suspicious. His *situpa* – his identification and pass – is so scuffed and folded it is unreadable, he has had no job before his present one – selling African art. Very shaky. Whorehound yells and snarls at him. The man stands utterly still, eyes flashing in the wayward light of the torch. We let him go.

'Magnanimous, eh,' grins Whorehound. 'Mag-fucking-nanimous. But what's the point?'

If my self-appointed mentor and protector sees no point, what are we doing here? The dark seems more threatening than ever. I cannot tell which is the more frightening: the aggression or the admission of helplessness.

At nine-thirty I finally bed down at Maleme, a thin green sleeping-bag under Matopos stars, naming constellations in a vague incantation to a different reality.

Days of unutterable boredom follow. We watch over the camp, throw berries at the 'zilards' that scurry across the warm rocks. Champing on pointlessness, Brinjal and I volunteer for a new Observation Post. We cook on an open fire; very clandestine. I express approval of the rat-packs. It is full moon. The dew is heavy in the night. We radio in every hour, 'November Tango Romeo [nothing to report]'. Sharp rocks niggle our spines. A herd of immaculate cattle wanders through our position. Is this a terr ruse to flush us out? Brinjal tries confusedly, mid-nightmare, to get out of bed in the deep of the night. A duiker thumps off in alarm. In the morning Empee and Meretrich are hung over from some party they managed to gate-crash. Brinjal whinges. We talk about God and the possible superiority of atheism as a philosophy. We can see nothing for trees and orange rocks from this OP. Brinjal whinges. We envy distant canoeists, having their holiday despite everything. We talk about the nature of women. *Hey, you guys, pack up, we're moving out, going to the hotel.* Brinjal cheers. We go on escort, drop off ambush sticks by moonlight, accost suspicious cyclists, miss another party. We talk about what we will be when we are big. I enjoy these conversations with Brinjal hugely. I realise that for all my air of self-containment, I lust for communication.

We lurk around base. Sterek is fuming because not he but Motherson has been given the chance of pursuing a group of 30 Communist Terrorists, CTs, 'terrs'. But there are rumours of another 42 coming in. (What do they mean, 'coming in'? Aren't they already *in*, just as we are *in*?) Sterek paces. There is a callout to some firing but it proves to be a Police Reserve night-shoot they didn't bother to publicise. 'The *dogs*,' fumes Whorehound. Someone performs an Accidental Discharge with his tinny G3 rifle and blows a small hole in the hotel ceiling and a somewhat bigger one in the asbestos roof.

But there is no action. Brinjal sighs down his gargantuan nose. He wants to get ambushed so he can have a decent crack at the enemy.

'Oh come on, Brinje, this savagery doesn't suit you,' I tell him. I feel protective towards him and his vulnerable nose and his gentle intelligence.

'Well, what the hell are we here for, then?'

'It just isn't authentic *you*.'

But I find myself wondering what 'authentic' means here. We are all becoming something we have not been before. All of us fantasise about that moment of *contact*, of wielding the lethal firepower placed in our boyish hands, anticipate that energising thrill of heroic terror.

But nothing is to happen to us, not yet. The holiday period over, and our first true Duty to Civilisation completed, we load the trucks, stutter and jerk in an ungainly convoy back to Llewellin, a moon of translucent quartz lipping over the flat horizon.

I hoard those fragments of beauty the way a man lost in a desert sucks on a stone for moisture.

It is difficult to valorise whatever it is we are being trained for.

* * *

I chafe continually at time wasted, inefficiency, disorganisation. Chats with the C Company trainee leaders make it clear how behind we are. 'Christ, what's the matter with you guys, we've been blowing up bridges, live battle drills . . .'. Men evicted from the Gwelo officers' course, trickling in, are appalled at Llewellin's lack of 'atmosphere': dirt and tin shambles, no discipline, no teamwork. The fundamental goal for most troopies is to 'cuff it' as much as possible. There are more frequent outbreaks of 'moggy' behaviour: setting fires under beds, fighting, throwing trunks out of windows. Glimpses of the 36-hour, non-stop, no-food-no-water initial selection course for the SAS – our élite – make us feel even more like bumbling peasants. 'In our present condition,' I reckon, 'we don't have a hope in hell of catching a fleeing terr.'

My own performance is worse. I am less fit than I thought. Tall has to give me extra drill instruction at night. What little shooting I get in is erratic. My double-tap skills – two rounds sent off in quick succession, before the recoil can disturb the aim – are particularly embarrassing. For some reason I am verbally abused by the Regimental Sergeant Major, a brick-coloured brute known as Moose. I mutter defensively into the diary:

> *I am both derided and left out – not that I really care that much; in these conditions I withdraw into myself and draw on internal reserves which I find far preferable – but it means I get the sort of jobs I'm doing right now, sitting on a runway guarding a tea urn while everyone else is practising battle drills.*

This at least gives me time to indulge my pessimism about the state of the country. Rather tenuously, I link this with the conduct of my comrades:

> *The other day Thompson swiped a plate of food from under a poor chap's nose while he was saying Grace. That's the height of contempt for belief, and perhaps typical of the world as a whole. I read the papers, and see the country slowly slipping, as a ceasefire becomes improbable and sanctions remain.*

And similarly:

> *Tractorback ('Aren't you the fucker who smashed my headlamp?') has taken over Fire Force – and immediately the system has run to seed. It just shows how important control from the top is, for the people, as it were, will never have the incentive or the initiative to organise themselves or listen to an equal who tries to. (Hence the unled platoon coming to blows yesterday over whether to march to the barrack-room or the graze-hall.) The same is happening at govern-*

ment level, where Hove, Co-Minister for Law and Order, has made statements he refuses to recant in the face of protests from Hilary Squires and General Walls (is the Army becoming more political?). This rift is complemented by clashes between ANC (Sithole) and UANC supporters – the first signs of civil war.

Our stomachs knot up as we are called to stand by at full alert: a 'riot scene' is rumoured to be brewing in Bulawayo's black townships. The scene is predicted for some reason to develop at 11 A.M. one Saturday. 'Nearer to civil war,' I note. Somehow, because a 'riot' is set in the streets rather than in the bush, it seems to us less 'military'. But aren't we *already* in the middle of a civil war? That's if one accepts the premise that we whites have become *bona fide* inhabitants of the country. The nationalists, perforce, have accepted no such thing.

We sit in the trucks and tap our rifle barrels with our thumbs, and talk.

'Fucking Communists are getting bolshy, ay.'

'Ag, they're just a lot of uneducated thickies with nothing better to do, you know.'

'Ja, dispensible.'

'I'm not looking forward to this, we aren't bloody policemen, we're being trained for the bush, mun.'

Thankfully, nothing happens.

4 April. US President Jimmy Carter has entirely rejected the Salisbury Agreement. Along with his earlier denouncement of any agreement entered into with Smith's government as illegal, including, one supposes, Kissinger's [cunning observation, this, but misdirected], he has made a solution by firepower the only way. I am gradually losing hope of the country staying on its feet. I am gradually losing hope of me staying in the country.

And a couple of days later I record the details of an interesting but fumbled RIC briefing on a recent Prime Minister's Conference with Army Commanders:

Ian Smith made it clear that the transition to majority rule was not made by choice, but forced via foreign pressure on South Africa.

Paradoxically, he says the decision to change was made 'a long time ago' i.e. 2 years, altogether too fast a transition for safety. On paper, the transition won't go too badly for the whites. God knows where I'd go if I ever had to leave Rhodesia . . .

The crunch will come when the constitution is referred by referendum to the population, that is, the present electorate. If we reject it, we've had it. If we don't, we may have had it anyway, since the war is likely to continue in either case.

And the war seems increasingly unwinnable. The RIC lecturer offers the somewhat meaningless but alarming calculation that to clear the guerrillas out of the country in a day, we would require 320 divisions.

We have the equivalent of *one division*.

Even in Llewellin, there are repeated warnings that the enemy is already in our midst, dark hints from Whorehound and others that there are at least two known guerrilla sympathisers working in camp, at another point six 'actual terrs'.

One morning we are scrambled hastily for a 'scene'. The more gung-ho whoop, others hunch into apprehensive silence. The scene proves to be roaring out just past Married Quarters to surround a nearby shanty village I didn't even know even existed. We swelter in the sun for two and a half hours while the place is searched. The prizes amount to one G3 rifle, some flare trip-wires, and seven scraps of stolen camo. Whorehound plays his usual games with his 9mm pistol, making the people – kids, women, youths – run gauntlets through the ranks of troopies. I am freshly disappointed in him.

'These are the people who are going to lose the country for us,' I gloomily record. 'One needs to be in the Army to appreciate just how deep-seated white racialism is.'

And in what way can I distinguish myself from my fellows, standing there, my feet stolidly planted, my FN at the ready? Can I be anything other than what I think I am, accomplice to a necessary evil?

* * *

With a certain amount of awe we watch the 106mm howitzers grumble past: new, polished, forbiddingly powerful, almost lithe on the backs of the high-chassis Unimog Two-Fives. The 'One-oh-six' embodies the military muscle we all wish we could hold in our own hands. If things come to the worst, if the T-55 tanks roll in across the borders, the 106 will turn the tide.

We are waiting, ranked on the backs of our armoured vehicles like rats on green logs, to depart for the final phase of our training. We've had our last weekend pass. Whorehound has grossly but somehow gently enquired for the last time, 'Get your end away this weekend, Arm?' We are embarking on a closing flurry of 'Battle Camps'. There are two phases to this grand euphemism for blisters and blundering: Classical Warfare and COIN (Counter-Insurgency).

The Class. War 'camp' is intended to prepare us for the 'real thing', under so-called 'conventional' conditions. The 106 howitzers are 'conventional'. The operation sprawls, boring and shaggily organised. Some 250 troopies swarm: the C Company trainee leaders, swaggering now in temporary stripes, the Signallers and the Drivers, the official cadets returned from Gwelo to harness us cannon-fodder to their budding leadership, an 'enemy' consisting partly of A Company, partly of Rhodesian African Rifles troops, and oddments of RAR's Demolition Squad. The last two are black men who have been in the Army for years. Now they have to succumb to the muddled, over-assertive commands of four-month white freshies.

Thirty k's north of Llewellin, on the granite crests of a mountain named Kholwani, we dig in in pairs. Clearly, being 'conventional' means being trained to wait to be killed on the spot. Pale granite shards splinter beneath our labouring picks. For the first time in a long while I am separated from Brinjal who has belatedly found his niche as a medic, has gone off to be interviewed for the course. So much for rebelling against his father, I chuckle to myself. I don't know if this move is a defeat or a triumph for him, but I know it will suit him, I am relieved, he will be safer. But I miss him, his clumsy innocent humour, his sad mincing gait.

Instead, I find myself bivvied with a Demolition Squad Ndebele named Patterson. This heavy-faced man I initially find to be irremediably dense and altogether too 'typical of his race'. He conforms to my stereotype of 'the general African taste in enjoyment: eating, sleeping and screwing'. After close proximity for a week, my impression is more nuanced, if patronising:

*Patterson and I talked about the things blacks always talk about –
sex, marriage, and money. Quite apart from the taints of traditional
African thinking, his thinking shows the usual black immaturity – he
wants a motorbike instead of a car, purely because it will bring him
more prestige – 'even the man with the car will look at me'. Mind you,
a lot of whites are the same. One thing that always impresses me is
the black man's logic. It may be short-sighted or immature or against
my principles, but it is always simple and direct, and my counter-
arguments are often too complex to explain well enough to convince
him. We get pretty het up – by the end of the exercise we had got to the
stage of friendship in which insults flowed freely, mostly good-natured.*

Why is Patterson fighting for the Rhodesians? Can't he get a better
job? His eyes go flat black. *Gandangas* – terrorists – murdered two
members of his family. They hacked his sister to death in front of
him. If he ever catches a gandanga, he will shove a stick of dynamite
into his rectum and blow him to pieces, he is in the Dem. Squad and
he will *demolish* the bastard. Race is only one of the issues in this war.
For some, it is not an issue at all.

Patterson and I have plenty of time to talk since the days are
spent sleeping and waiting for 'the enemy' to assault 'our' hill and
noisily slaughter us in our trenches. We hear the 106s pounding away
in the distance; the sound brings a thrill to our manly hearts. We lust
to see them in action. At night, we can see the distant lights of
Llewellin's notorious No.3 Guard, and the amber glow of Bulawayo
on the undersides of the low clouds, an obscurely reflected promise
of warmth and ease.

The nights are largely expended, though, on sundry futile exercises. Early on, as I wander through the kitchen area at the bottom of
the hill in search of ever-elusive graze, I am commandeered by a
couple of the officer cadets to help them out on a night 'recce' of
somebody or other's farmhouse base. 'A total disaster,' I sum up. On a
subsequent night, we execute our 'strategic withdrawal'; under yet
another pseudo-corporal. In near-pitch darkness we stumble down
the hill, establish the platoon rendezvous in the wrong place, blunder in a long line towards another rendezvous where the two companies
marry up, with continuous stopping and starting for reasons lost in
the starlight. A two-hour truck-journey, debus, deploy into a 'gonk

posi' for a meagre three hours' sleep before beginning a two-day 'advance to contact'. That is, we go back to where we started from.

The highlight – 'if there could be said to be a highlight' – is a final night assault on the Kholwani farm buildings. We advance across the abandoned fields in an impossibly straight line, as Icarus flares pop into blinding life above us and bathe the scene in a synthetic moonlight. Sobered by our vulnerability, we plod doggedly on, storm the position at the last moment with an assortment of falsely demonic yells, and finally, like Wilfred Owen's soldiers, 'turn our backs on the haunting flares' and stumble back to bed. The whole thing feels, I imagine, rather like a brief and uninteresting assault on some grimy, faceless and unresponsive prostitute.

And we never do get to see the 106.

Much later, my ever-resourceful father will procure one of the massive, perforated 106 cartridge-cases, chromium-plate it, top it with a copper-tipped aluminium head, and make of it a lamp which stands, uneasily elegant, in my bedroom. By such subterfuges of artistry we domesticate our wars.

A couple of days back in barracks allow me to record a snippet of otherworldly news:

> *The Executive Committee is now appealing to the populace for support, as though it were an imposed thing, as in many ways it is; also that the price of petrol is up 14c a unit* [the unit of rationing], *fresh indication of how the economy is failing. The main consideration is now to get as much as possible out of this Army stint in terms of practical living experience . . . to try everything.*

It all seems so hopeless. Rumours float around our ears like clouds of elusive gnats. Our training promises nothing more concrete than disintegrating feet and grass-seeds in our balls. I snatch at a broader idealism of personal growth for some kind of purpose to my being there, some salve and salvation.

We are plunged straight back into the suffocating maelstrom of the last phase of COIN exercises. They have called it 'Operation Weary Trooper'. Intended to prepare us for real guerrilla-war conditions, this feels rather more probable than the Class. War nonsense. 'Weary Trooper' is about right: a fortnight of sodden gloom relieved by erratic flurries of activity. We rumble out to Tagwala Dam in the Matopos National Park, a bumpy roundabout route in the armour-sided Crocodiles through Galati Tribal Trust Land, with Khumalo TTL to the south – an area apparently 'totally subverted'. (As it well might be, given that Khumalo is the original Ndebele clan-name, the royal family from Zululand, the bloodline of Mzilikazi and Loben-gula themselves.) This shoulder-jostling ride in the high-sided trucks is becoming familiar, the comforting heavy feel of layered sandbags beneath our feet, the dramatic, communal clash of breech-blocks as we leave Bulawayo's suburbs and load the serried FNs. And every-where, our most intimate badge, the Army's camouflage: the simple dark-green-and-olive of the vehicles, the green, brown and beige chunky streakiness of our uniforms, as distinctive in its patterns as the US Marines', Brit, or Tanzanian camo.

Sixty k's out of 'Skies' – Bulawayo – we debus, and begin a squelching eight-kilometre walk in to a farmhouse base. Meretrich has been designated our stick leader: distracted by his own irrepress-ible jokes, he loses the compass, leads us up the wrong tributary, cannot assert his authority. We radio in a false position and race to cover our error. Nearer the farmhouse, we find Borrish and Tractor-back setting up an elaborate 'jungle lane' with pop-up targets; I look forward with some trepidation to this test of our quick-kill shooting, our double-taps. Tractorback looks at me suspiciously: 'Aren't you the fucker who . . . ?'

Brinjal is back to complete the basic training, before he goes to medics. He doesn't talk about having a crack at the enemy any more, just wants all this nonsense to be over so he can start stitching people up. Deployed in a defensive perimeter in the thorn-scrub around the farmhouse, he and I chip our shallow shell-scrapes in the terracotta earth, thankful for the moonlight that has replaced the sunset, col-lapse into them, wrapped only in our bivvies to keep the dew off. In the night, it rains coldly. That apparently kiln-fired earth turns to slush; the scrapes fill with blind sludge. We scarcely dare turn in our soddenness for fear of losing what tentative warmth we can gener-ate. Still drizzling down in the morning. Brinjal stands miserably beside the spineless bivvy. His uniform clings to his shivering shoulders; his long nose is accentuated by drips of rain and despair; he sags from the eyebrows down. He stares at his boots. The mood catches. I stare at my boots. It keeps on drizzling. We stare at our boots. And after a bit the absurdity of this set-up dawns on us, seizes us irrepressibly in the intestines. We dissolve in paroxysms of insane giggles.

Samuel Beckett would have loved it. There hasn't been a miserable situation since then when I haven't been hugely cheered by the memory of Brinjal standing in the Matabeleland rain, caked with misery, staring at his boots.

While some platoons are off into Khumalo to execute fully operational Observation Posts, we dogsbodies as usual remain as the malleable manpower on whom the officer cadets practise their tactical skills. Now it is a three-day 'ambush' succeeded by a 'follow-up'. The ambush is a 'Horlicks' (another of our substantial fund of obscure synonyms for a cock-up). Our gaunt and imprecise cadet-commander muddles his orders, extracts us too late, leaves us on the saddle of the wrong *gomo*, goes off to recce and never comes back. All about as clandestine as a mobile circus. McGinnagin is there, launching noisily into some indecipherable Pictish epic. Hamerkop is enjoying himself hugely, sharpening his wit at Digger Potatohead's expense. The cadets are quarrelling furiously over who is likely to end up with what rank, the loudest being a burly American, booming, incisive, and unpopularly harsh – a vagrant from the US Army.

During the day I sleep further, write up 'characters', design a house. Domestic creativity feels as remote and alluring as a Mediterranean jacuzzi. Brinjal and I fantasise endlessly about the future. We'll run a café in deepest Patagonia. Or a brothel in Van Diemen's Land. Or he'll become a doctor after all and I'll write best-selling novels based on the most disgusting secrets of his patients. We talk as if we don't understand that we'll soon be parted.

Eventually moving into a night stop-group posi, we shiver in a rapier cold, slapping at squadrons of mosquitoes, and generally alerting our potential ambushees to our presence with rustles, coughs, and a symphony of snores. The night is enlivened only by three bush-babies skipping light as blue-grey feathers through the muhacha branches overhead, a promise of something more gentle and sane.

We hear the tumult of the ambush finally being initiated in the distance. Our stop-group isn't called upon to stop anyone.

In the morning we embus, the lead vehicle 'hits a landmine'; we 'follow-up', executing a grimly plodding hairpin through boulder-strewn thickets and waist-deep vlei grass, and finally assault the 'enemy position' across a narrow valley. Pouring some 1300 rounds into the anonymous bush, we score a grand twelve hits on the pre-positioned targets. The war is temporarily halted while we extinguish a fire started up by tracers in the grass. McGinnagin dribbles the dregs of his waterbottle on the flames and goes to sleep upwind of the acrid smoke while we flail with msasa branches. We spend an hour or two recovering the doppies, because, as Whorehound puts it, 'the cattle pick them up and find it difficult to pass through their teats'.

In the middle of the final night exercise, things appear to take a more exciting turn – though none of us are really sure whether we're out on a real scene or not. Four or five insurgents are reported to be taking 40 recruits out through the Maleme corridor. (In our muddled mythology, these recruits are always coerced, but are judged to have received their just deserts when shot.) The pursuit is called off. 'The *dogs*,' Whorehound snarls, and trucks us in surly silence back to barracks.

Our camouflage pants are worn satisfactorily pale and mature at the knees, though it is hard to say quite what we have learned.

And we never do get a crack at the jungle lane.

* * *

The end is nigh: we have some 24 hours to prepare for the Open Day and the passing-out parade. The prospect of a five-day pass seems like the promise of a belly-dancer bearing wine and succulent veal. Parents are coming to see their heroic offspring pass out, including my father, who has driven right across the country to carry his own flesh-and-blood home. In between trying to deal with two weeks' mud-spattered kit, dusty barrack-rooms, and heaps of rubbish, revelry erupts. Some impatient troopies attempt to go AWOL for the night, one gets caught. There is an additional charge that our drill is up to shit and the barracks a pigsty.

The five-day pass is cancelled.

We don't get even a snifter of the passing-out parade.

My father is predictably furious. With rubicund Ulster bluntness he rages at the CO, threatening repercussions via some brigadier friend of his. The institution is unmoved. My father goes home alone, having had only the meagre consolation of competing against me in a range shoot.

'Can you shoot, Arm?' Whorehound asks me nastily.

'I can get a two-inch grouping as easily as anyone,' I lie.

I get the grouping, my double-taps are good, but my father still wins.

That the 'major inspection' turns out to be a two-minute glance across the bedcovers confirms our suspicions that the whole thing is a hypocritical frame-up to obtain manpower for No.3 Guard.

'Fuck! If they need people to guard the fucking ammo dump, why can't they just say so?' Meretrich has a particularly juicy way of saying *Fuck*.

22 May. My nineteenth birthday. No.3 Guard. Pre-dawn watch. Two hours of lancing cold alone atop one of four towers of open mesh, no protection from the wind but what you wear. We've done this before, several times, brooding over the floodlit humps of earth in which our brass-and-cordite *matériel* slumbers, trying to distinguish sheep from saboteurs, singing to the illusory warmth of Bulawayo's quivering lights. Now, demoralised, no one gives a toss, including the clueless cor-porals, a couple of arbitraries from Brady Barracks. Coloureds, to boot. Now that is a *real* index of our demotion. We are up there in our metal cages with biscuits and blankets, carelessly dozing as the dawn mist closes in.

Training ends not with a bang but with a series of muted whim-pers and ragged cheers as sections of the company clear their kit and trickle away for a skeletal pass before joining their units. Whore-hound is leaving Llewellin, too, 'going operational', he tells me with a smirk. He makes me feel privileged to know this. 'You take *fucking* good care of yourself, you hear! You dog.' And he lifts his lip in that familiar wolfish snarl; but I realise, with a start, that he has actually grown fond of me. He pats me roughly on the shoulder with a hand like a side of pork, and is gone.

Brinjal comes over from the Medical Training School to say good-bye, too, shaking my hand with his usual ridiculous formality and restraint. I am not sure if I will ever see him again. There ought to be a happier end than this, if it is an end. It is, perhaps, the first inkling

I have that this isn't a novel I am living, but a sequence of disjointed encounters with no obvious purpose at all.

I seem to be amongst the last to leave. I have to pay $2 for a bivvy-cover I hadn't been issued with; I have to contribute damages for a platoon piss-up I didn't attend; I have to help mop up the rice-flecked spatters of curry-coloured vomit from the floor of the ransacked Club.

And then, unspectacularly, I am out of there, gratefully putting the soulless shambles of Llewellin forever behind me.

Or so I think.

* * * * *

PART 2

Living Leaves

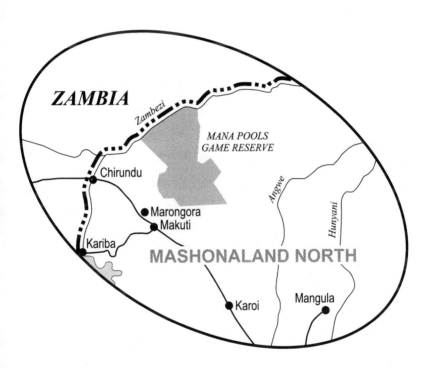

Chapter 4

Rhino Elysium

He sauntered back from the polished barrack
To the seething streets and luxurious
Pavements, the swaggering rookie raw and black
With sun and mud, full of his furious
Uniform, stable belt and rakish beret.
He has set his smile and walk to charm,
His tongue to offhand stories of the fray,
But found the war too far gone, people too calm
And knowing for him to be new. Boldly
He whistled his high morale, and at the corner
Bumped a sergeant, tattered cockade and denims worn
Through at the knees, who cursed him coldly.

THE TRUCK is beginning to sway from side to side through msasa-wooded hills. The wind is in my hair, a warm roaring; the world smells green despite the June dryness of winter.

And there in the distance, an elephant, imperturbable in its wrinkled bulk, strips its lunch from a black acacia. My spirit lifts.

We have left the farmlands of Sinoia and Karoi behind us and, heading northwards, enter the wooded labyrinths of the Zambezi escarpment. Our tracking course will be taking place at Mana Pools, on the Zambezi River itself. It is the northernmost point of the country, the outermost frontier, pure wilderness. I grip the rollbar, contain my eagerness. My eyes water in the wind.

These hills make my heart lurch with recognition. Though I was born on the barely undulating plains of Bulawayo, I was raised in the Vumba mountains of the Eastern Highlands. Forest and rock are intrinsic to my well-being. Steep slopes anywhere excite me. I was in the French Alps once, at Chamonix. I was awestruck by the view from the dizzying cable-car station on the Aiguille du Midi, the gleaming shoulder of Mont Blanc to my right, the improbable spike of the Matterhorn 70 k's away across a fantasial but brittle panorama, beneath me nothing but blond rock, ice of unapproachable blue, and a solitary raven coasting across the glaciers. But I also felt spurned, a bedraggled salesman of mere blood at a parade of frigid and timeless queens.

The Vumba mountains are less spectacular than the Alps, but they are *alive*. Their domed batholiths breathe, roughly pelted with amiable greens. Miombo woodland blushes into copper and crimson and luminous lime in spring. On the lower slopes, evergreen forests soar 30 metres into filigreed, bird-impassioned canopies, damp with the odours of centuries, massive as Yggdrasil the World-tree, moss-baized, motherly. These mountains are moody, more complex than concertos, every crest and gully potent with surprise.

Approaching the Zambezi Valley, it feels, for a space, almost as if I am coming home.

We pause at Marongora, the National Parks station perched on the edge of the escarpment. Looking northwards, I find the levelled expanse of the Valley forbidding, Amazonian. Maybe 40 k's away, the intermittent tinsel of the great river reflects sunlight. The Zambian hills beyond it are as intangible as a smoky bruise.

Enemy territory.

While we wait for an escort to Mana Pools itself, we go in search of a lion's claw.

A ranger drives us, *his* impromptu escort, down the escarpment, north along the main road to the river, to Chirundu. This once-thriving sugar-cane centre on the Zambezi is long-abandoned, the signboards tattered with gunfire, the Motel's windows shattered. Petrol-pumps spill their innards onto grass-starred paving. At the deserted police station, rotting sandbags release wan pyramids of sand. The Army base overlooking the Otto Beit suspension bridge is equally decrepit, the gate unattended. An empty beerbottle winks russet in the guardhouse. A few languid, unshod soldiers shuffle out to greet us.

The war, evidently, is elsewhere.

The dead owner of the claw is a black-maned male lion, shot

through the head by a troopie who was out collecting firewood. Lucky shot, with a mere FN.

'Probably just curious,' says the ranger, prodding the body. Blood trickles from a nostril, the guts stink in a purple heap on one side. 'Not man-eating material, he's in good nick.'

The skin would fetch $2000, reckons the ranger, and the missing claw, stolen while the body was strung up from a tree for the night, $80. Everybody denies knowledge. We load the corpse onto the Puma, the ranger's Labrador barking and hiding, the bullterrier gnawing at the hard muscle.

Back at Marongora, a porcine straw-hatted American hunter (some of the Hunting Areas are still, despite everything, open to tourists) poses for his red-lipped wife's camera, rifle in hand, his foot on the dead lion's neck. I curl my lip, thinking, *Tub of fraudulent lard.*

Already, this all feels so different from the Army I have known. I warm to these rangers, their neat but motley clothes, their informality, their enthusiasm for the wild for its own sake. They will be our bosses for the duration of the tracker course, and I like the prospect. They are not exactly removed from the war: they participate fully, even courageously. But they are bigger than the war. They revel in a life-force greater than any mere political squabble.

Or so I want to believe.

One ranger daunts, disturbs, attracts me. We cross paths only once at Marongora. A long, close-cropped head sways above us, pale blue eyes flicker, rest on mine for a moment. Mobile lips twitch in the merest beginning of a smile, sardonic or welcoming it is difficult to say. Hands like a pianist's, big as Rachmaninov's, powerful and sensitive and still. This man carries an air of calm, of self-possession, which I immediately envy. Then he vanishes.

Our escort vehicle arrives: the Pookie. None of us have seen one before, we swarm around it, the driver explains its features. It detects landmines, and is one of the niftier strokes of make-do engineering produced in the Rhodesian war. Its VW engine perches on the stripped chassis; its innards are all on the outside like a mobile fragment of the Pompidou Centre. The driver wedges himself into a minimalist, bulbous, horrendously cramped and armoured cab.

The rangers joke, 'You better cut down on the beers, Archie, you'll never get yourself out of that mincing-machine again!'

Archie looks like the Archbishop Makarios. He grins through a yellow beard.

'You berra be grateful, you fuckin' Zookeepers. What's the betting my li'l peepers pick up a landmine on your road today?' And he lowers the winglike trays of metal-detecting gear, horizontal between the fat smooth Formula One tyres. The tyres' weight-to-surface-area ratio is so low it can run over landmines without detonating them.

'I can run across your foot without detonating that, either,' Archie grins.

'This bloody dragonfly couldn't pick up a whore if it tried,' a ranger taunts.

'It'll pick up a nail at 50 k's an hour, china!'

We load flapping boxes of food and clanking trunks aboard the Puma. With shrieking brakes we descend the tumbling folds of the escarpment, turn right, and pound off along the Mana road. We have to sit perched on the bags of mealie-meal and collapsing piles of *katundu*, in defiance of all sensible anti-landmine procedures. We have 80 k's of gravel road to negotiate to Mana, every patch of oddly scumbled earth potentially hides a mine. We crouch on our boxes and put our faith entirely in Archie and the Pookie.

'We're National Service, we're scum of the earth,' moans Meretrich. 'What does it matter if we're blown to bits?'

'Beautiful country for ambushes,' I also observe nervously: thick mopani scrub, clotted forest along dry river beds where we have to slow to a crawl over the narrow, sway-backed bridges. One of the Mana rangers, a burly, squinting blond with a voice like a mild lager, points out the bridge the gooks tried to blow, the spot where so-and-so was 'pulled', the patch of worried earth where a mine was detonated in April. For some reason, he giggles. But there has been no other action since Christmas. Mana itself hasn't been revved since 1976.

Dust-caked, evening light falling about us in ruby swathes, we are conducted by the ranger Lager around Mana camp. Unprotected, neatly-kept, it lies spreadeagled amongst great *Acacia albida* trees. Our National Service quarters, 30 metres from the river-bank, consist of two prefab rondavels under a thatched canopy, small kitchen and bathroom buildings out back. Our home for the next six months.

'And you'd better keep it *pristine*. Or Tim will string you up from a leadwood.' Tim?

By night we will sleep on stretchers wedged into odd corners of 'Fort Mana', a low-slung, four-square construction of concrete blocks. Heavy-roofed turrets guard the corners; another looms over the top. A frail radio mast quivers in the wind, our only contact with the outside. A buzzing generator provides electricity. A little shrubbery has been introduced here and there, as a token of wildness or of domesticity it is impossible to say. Only the chief ranger has a tiny room of his own, filled with books, a typewriter perched on a narrow desk. 'No one goes in there. Ever.'

In this grey labyrinthine laager, at 2 A.M. this first of many nights, I take my nervous turn at guard, two hours of soft-padded pacing. Peering out through the turrets' slots into the intricate dark, I take what comfort I can from knowing that, between the fence and the fort walls, electrically-activated Addams-grenades, stick-mounted devices lethal up to 200 metres, offer some protection. Depending on which turret I'm in when the attack comes, I can snatch up an MAG, or a heavy-barrelled FN, or a two-inch mortar. Out of sight in the black, insect-cradled night, hyenas giggle and whoop as they ransack the trash-cans in the deserted scout quarters, and hippos honk sonorously on the river.

* * *

At six in the morning the sun is up and the winter air merely cool. We are lined up on the patch of dust they call the parade-ground. We have no weapons yet, can't tell how seriously to take this.

The African game-scouts snap to attention.

'Here's the Main Manna,' whispers Meretrich.

It is the tall, self-contained ranger I saw at Marongora. His pale eyes rest on us for a slow second, seem to dismiss us as irrelevant. He returns the game-scouts' crisp salutes with a perfunctory gesture, issues their instructions for the day in flawless Shona. Finally he turns to us. We stiffen, conscious suddenly of a presence of extraordinary sinew. He stands for a moment, lightly poised on legs noticeably bowed but solid as seasoned marante, frosted with fine blond hair. Yellow slip-slops detract not at all from an air of natural authority. His skull is harshly narrow, the clean-shaven face a gaunt version of T.E. Lawrence, the eyes chipped aquamarine. The long upper lip is curled and expressive, hovers somewhere between sensitivity and cynicism.

In some lonely part of my being, I know that I have been looking for a role model, a hero, someone both like and different from my father. My hero must be a door into a manhood of my own choosing. I find myself wondering if this is the man. It feels right to be a little afraid of one's hero. At the same time, I sense a chink of approachability in this honed ranger's armour.

'I'm Tim Boot, the chief ranger here. You can call me Tim. That doesn't mean you can give me any crap.' But there's an ambiguous twitching at the corner of his mouth.

The other rangers arrive at a canter – Lager, Gdansk, Humbleman. They are in full uniform today, and bashful. 'Sorry we're late, Tim.'

And another individual, black-haired, brown, built like the proverbial brick shithouse. He strolls up with a kind of relaxed and calculating insolence. Invincible calves bulge above tractor-tyre sandals. His khaki shirt hangs out, his eyes are concealed behind designer shades.

Tim grates, 'As for you, you disreputable ponce, you'll be late for your own funeral.' But he is laughing behind the stringy muscles of his face.

'I can't believe you still do all this military shit. You call this a parade? And who are all these wankers?'

This is, we learn, a Selous Scout friend of Tim's, on holiday between crazy raids into deep Mozambique. His idea of a break is to conduct a war of words and physical exertion against his best mate in the middle of a remote bush camp.

'Obstacle course today, is it?' he taunts. 'I'm gonna whip your bony ass.'

And they go at it. The contest is affectionate but unyielding, laced with verbal insult, never-ending. Later, we will see cross-country pack runs (The Scout boasts he takes his craps without removing his 50-kilo pack), shooting, arm-wrestling, even a joke contest, these mismatched rivals cheerfully attempting to grind one another into exhaustion. As for the assault course this particular morning, The Scout is agile, determined, and fleet of foot – but it is the grim and shanky Tim Boot who lopes to the finish first.

This is admirable, but it isn't what attracts me. Tim Boot seems to wear his bone and tendon on the outside, but I recognise a tenderness beneath it, even perhaps a fundamental loneliness to mirror my own. But for now, we are merely 'NS'. There are three 'Old NS', still here from the last intake of tracker trainees. They enjoy a touch more status. But we 'New NS', six raw, incompetent rookies, are mere excrescences, fit only for camp hack work. As Meretrich said, 'scum of the earth'.

Tim Boot ends our first parade harshly, implacably. 'By the way, there will. Be. No. Tracking course. You are here to patrol the Park. Chete.'

And he strides away, leaving us numbed and shuffling.

* * *

We seethe at this betrayal.

'I'm going to complain to the Director, that's for sure, he can't do this to us, he's just a pisswilly ranger . . .'.

'I think I'm going to apply for SAS, Scouts even, bugger me if I'm going to sit on my arse here doing stuff-all, we need to be useful, mun!'

I contemplate asking my father to contact his brigadier friend, pull some strings. Our anger is deepened by Tim Boot's cold aloofness. He tells magnificent, expertly dramatised jokes in the fort at night, but this serves only to make us less sure of him. Our standing is not improved when (ironically on one of the rare occasions when he wanders into the NS quarters apparently just for a chat) he idly picks up one of my little black diaries, indiscreetly left lying on the rondavel wall. Before I can object, he reads aloud its opening sentence:

As usual when boredom creeps over, the blokes scandalise, criticise. Today Tim's the primary subject, suffering multiple charges of neglect (such as not telling us before that he had a volley-ball net), and a couldn't-give-a-damn attitude (such as too-long patrols), even downright hatred, disgust and contempt (of NS).

Tim clamps his narrow jaw even tighter, and sends us out to cut down leadwood trees for the next four days. Sobered, we grumble: our idle chatter was surely symptomatic of no more than a pettiness that has set in with time, with isolation, with loss of perspective. 'How can he take it so seriously, he's mull!'

'You stupid bastard,' Meretrich flings at me, 'look what you've done now, I'm going to burn those bloody diaries of yours, they're illegal anyway.'

There is more surly talk of rebellion, of leaving.

My own desire to escape is rapidly overtaken by its opposite: to stay there for the whole of my National Service. Mana Pools is beginning to exert its complex spell of unforgettable magnificence. Within weeks I am fingering forms to apply to join National Parks proper, tortuously balancing this against my ambition to go to university. All previous plans and goals unravel. I am overwhelmed with the desire to settle deeply into this place.

At this point, in the second half of 1978, Mana has not been vitiated by a tourist presence for years. The herds of elephant and buffalo have been left unculled and unmolested. All but the main access road has been overgrown or trampled into the summer muds; the lodges at Mucheni and Vundu Point are in total disrepair. The doorway of one still bears the scars of an AP mine that blew a ranger's foot off.

Otherwise, it is the natural that governs here. Lions loll in forbidding tawny repose just a few paces downriver. Elephants pad through the middle of camp with mountainous bones and their age-less calm. Ground hornbills boom us awake in the mornings, warthogs trot with comical verve. Mambas haunt the thickets of creeper shadowing the great leadwoods. Out in the green mopane woodlands, kudu watch, ears wide with soft caution. After rain, red spiders frost the heavy-scented earth. The nights are operatic with insects and frogs.

And always the great river, its greased implacable surge, shifting sandbanks ribbed with dank crocodiles, cool algae, raucous geese, translucent fish that flock to nibble your skin when you squat in the olive shallows.

Few people, apart from the men who have made the protection of these places their living, can have had the extraordinary privilege of encountering, week after week, at arm's length, such an abundance of wildlife. It is as close as I have got in my life to the timelessness of an Elysium. It is not some mythical heaven – an Eden devoid of viol-ence or danger – but it is a world that governs itself entirely without us, only waxing and waning as the seasons shift from dry winter to sodden summer, and back.

Poetry becomes possible again. My diary entries stumble towards a recognition that beauty, as Mies van der Rohe said of God, is in the details:

A classic early summer pattern: a half-mooned, clear morning sky building up into cloud with the air pressing down thick and sweaty, thunder bumbling over Zambia. Then, come afternoon, a bucketing damp wind, spitting spats of rain, then sleeping down into a blanket of ruckled cloud yellow at the edges with sullen storm, and the air cloying again under the arms and the curves of the throat. It will not rain, but will pass and clear a fevered sky with a taut cloth of brassy sun.

In the night, in the shrine of the crickets' tap and surge, skirl and burr, the whoop and clear giggles of the hyena, the high squeak of the water dikkop, the elephants snap trees and the hippos clash and roar in the river. The white stars prick the stippled clouds yellow-grey in a falling full moon.

The need to match words to details surfaces in me compulsively, unstoppably. I am desperate to write myself into a different future. Strenuously I imitate the style of Gerard Manley Hopkins's journals – half-despairingly, too, knowing that Hopkins is overwhelming my own voice. But what *is* my own voice?

At every spare moment I escape the often hilarious but abrasive racket of the other NS. Feeling at once too solitary and at home, I spend hours on the rippled sandbanks or among the great acacias beyond the camp edge, writing, sketching, just watching: the nerv-ous wiry impala, the circling bateleurs, a solitary old baboon:

An exile sulks in his sage days,
Some gloom of battled retirement
Dragging
A tatter of swagger . . .

Throng-
Less leader, youth-dark rejected
Into muzzle-smudged grey, he drinks
A long,
A lonely life,
Uncompanioned strife
without
a song.

I am propped one evening against the ridged trunk of a mopani, watching elephants so close I can sketch the textures of the backs of their languid trunks, when I become aware of the softest of movements behind me. Gone almost rigid with fear that some jaundiced, red-eyed jumbo has snuck up to stamp me into the dust, I turn my head with infinitesimal care.

Tim Boot is looking down at my sketch-pad. 'You're good,' he breathes. 'D'you paint?'

'A bit. I've got water-colours here.'

'Do one of Long Pool for me. I'll pay you.' He walks away, the long hunting rifle aslant across his indomitable back.

I have never been more nervous about showing a painting in my life. I take it up to the fort one night. Maybe the dull light in there will blur its flaws. Tim gazes at it a long time, angled to the lamp, his long head as predatory as a marabou's. My heart labours through his silence. Then he turns away and rummages in a bag. 'How much did you want?'

'Ag, no, look –'

'Twenty.' He shoves the bill in my shirt pocket. And abruptly, as if he wants the conversation over and done with, 'D'you write, too? Other than scurrilous diary entries that is.' The long upper lip is twitching.

I shrug, flushed. 'A bit. Do you?'

He seems startled I should have the temerity to ask. 'I write reports to headquarters.'

He waves me away. The tenuous connection made, he ignores me. This exchange is not, evidently, to be thought of as a bonding moment. Over the weeks I watch him, half repelled, half intrigued. I write in the diary of *his habit of stroking the pale hairs of his forearm against the grain, over and over. How his thin, mobile lips writhe with an amusement that never breaks out into laughter. His dramatisations: brilliant jokester. How the other rangers chaff with him, hiding their fear of him behind their bared teeth. How his observations can rake across our sensitivities; I can't tell if he is ashamed or enamoured of his well-timed cruelties. He makes everything we say seem obvious and thin; his intelligence now laced with some bitterness, now relieved by a strange compassion.*

Most importantly for me, Tim reads – good stuff – and talks about his reading. He finds me reading Steinbeck. He humbles me with the trenchant immediacy of his reaction. 'Have you read *East of Eden*? That Cathy! You just want to crawl in between the pages and beat that woman to a pulp,' he fumes. Many years later, I will catch myself reacting much the same way, even using that same phrase, of Jason in Faulkner's *The Sound and the Fury*, surely one of the most despicable characters in literature. We are all, in some ways, patchwork people, built up of conscious and unconscious mimicries of the words and gestures of those who impress us.

Urged on by Meretrich's inverse snobbery, we also read junk: Robert Early's Rhodesian war-novel, *A Time of Madness*. Early was once the manager of Makuti Motel, near Marongora. Tim and I agree that his novel, like almost all white Rhodesian fiction apart from Doris Lessing, is appalling. Early has his heroes trupping at an impossible eleven kph – through jesse, the thickest imaginable bush! – and hanging by their climactic fingertips over the abyss of Victoria Falls.

Meretrich bellows, 'No, this is the stuff! This is the mainstream. It's racy, it's easy, you make money, why write all those big words for about six people?'

And Tim says soberly, 'No, you're right. This is the stuff we have to live for. Escape. We have to have the story. In life there's no story. There's no narrative. Only chaos.'

There are also moments when Tim Boot is capable of impressing even his sturdiest critics. Some of us go out with him on a buffalo hunt: meat is needed for all these red-blooded men. On the back of the truck we bounce across the hoof-pocked flood plain until we find a victim trailing behind a small herd.

'That one, she's not well,' says Tim. He is training a game scout to hunt; the scout botches the shot; the buffalo canters away, moaning.

'Follow, but not too close.' Tim leaps down and begins to run. He runs the buffalo down for four kilometres, tenacious as a burr, then, just as she is about to plunge irretrievably into the Zambezi, hardly breaking his loping stride he shoots her cleanly up the anus.

Back at camp the rough black corpse is skinned and stripped to the bone.

'Damn, no wonder she was slow, she was pregnant.' The little foetus spills from the sinewed, translucent sac, its wrinkled muzzle pink as a puppy's, the tiny hooves a rubbery lime-green. Tim squats by it, too long, the knuckles of his thumbs pressed against his forehead, as if he were praying. When he rises his pale face is rigid, his temples marbled with wrestling veins. He walks quickly away.

'Jesus, what's his case?' mutters Wastrel, 'she woulda been vulture-food eventually anyway.'

None of us knows quite how to take Tim Boot.

Except maybe Bullock, whose opinion is succinct and irreversible: 'He's just a strip of biltong dipped in shit, that's what.'

Maybe Bullock is right, really, given all the donkey-work Tim gives us. In between patrols, we yawningly guard our visitors' aircraft on the distant dirt airstrip, or clear the elephants off it before they land, whitewash the buildings, load firewood, laboriously shred dead animals into biltong. Least interesting of all is doing 'transects'. We actively resent this labour-intensive method of determining animal population densities. It involves taking scat samples over kilometres of floodplain, marking off a metre square every ten metres, and noting what bits of dung have been deposited in that square. Someone will then use a complicated formula to arrive at a population estimate. At least we learn to recognise dozens of varieties of turd.

It is the nearest we get to a tracking course.

One day I ask Tim Boot, 'Why exactly is it that you've refused to do the tracking course with us?'

To my astonishment, he has started to invite me out to walk with him. Maybe because I've asked him about this or that bird or plant, he has decided I'm worth something. The other NS mock this development, but I go with him. My short legs have a hard time keeping up with his tireless lope. He begins to teach me things, to read the dung, how to ring the fish eagle chick whose nest we climb to, the Shona names of the trees and grasses. We joke about the others back in camp, set off one another's dramatic streak, mimic them mercilessly: Bullock's saturnine frown, Meretrich's donkey-like bray of laughter, Wastrell's lank hair and speech impediment and wide flat feet.

Now he looks at me sidelong. 'Are you even vaguely aware of what's going on out there?'

'What do you mean?'

'The political scenario is over. This is the endgame. You could be out of the Army by December. There will be a surrender within the year, mark my words. Why the devil do you want to put yourself into the line of fire now? I'm certainly not about to do that for you. I'd rather you stayed here and got stomped on by an elephant than got yourselves shot for a dumb, misconceived, lost cause. You guys are so young, so stupid, so full of the delusions of Smith propaganda. The longer this war goes on, the more bitter the aftermath will be, the less secure your future here will be. We must have our majority government and have it soon and just get over it and start the healing. Heal, just heal. There's been too much pain, just too much.'

I hesitate. 'You have some specific pain in mind?'

But he does not reply, looks distant, begins to walk again along the edge of Long Pool. 'This spiky stuff, they call *dindindere* . . . Astonishing blue flower in March.'

Tim ruffles my loyalties, makes me rethink my every assumption. But he also shows me how to live in the present, observe. He teaches me to make fire in the ancient manner, with a baseplate of ironwood, a rolling-stick of *munyami* monkey-finger, a sprinkling of elephant-dung. We fashion string from baobab bark, chewing stiff fibre until our jaws ache, rolling the string on our reddened thighs. He shows me that you can cut an eighteen-inch section of the square-barked *renje* vine for water, and carve the twigs of Zambezi ebony, *mashumbadombo*, into fishhooks and arrowheads. Mopani makes good firewood because of its turpentine content; it conceals sweet larvae under its leaves, mopani-bee honey in the fissured bark, edible squirrels in the hollows. The burned leaves of *damba* leave salt if you strain the ash through grass, and the chewed sticks of *pfenje* are your

71

home-from-home aphrodisiac. 'Your pointing stick goes hunting!' Tim laughs. He actually laughs.

* * *

Nothing is more more unique about our time at Mana than our close encounters with rhino. It really is Rhino Elysium: hardly a single patrol is completed without at least one or two sightings.

11 June. Close brush with rhino last night, moving into our sleeping position in the close moonlight. Mother and calf. Game scout Chawada, up front, rattles his rifle, and Oxenfeck whistles and snorts at them, while we five are loosening pack straps and choosing our trees. Chawada and Oxy start backing up, and five little soldiers vanish down the path in a blur of starlight. Eventually Mother goes left and Junior right, and we sneak nervously in between. I bring up the rear – walking backwards.

21 June. Last night. The last taint of daylight across the Zambezi, the moon still down but paling the sky. We're bedding down in an area of dry jesse bush, brittle, thorned. There comes a rhino, breaking through the sticks, snaffling close. Game scout Small throws sticks into the dusk. Emsburt urinates in its general direction, as that seemed to chase off the last one. Rhino is unimpressed, snorts. Heavy trampling. The boys scatter like startled baboons. Small and I stop to listen. Unaware that the rhino is crackling off and round to the right, the others continue scrambling for trees.

Laptop is scuttling back and forth wondering how he's going to climb a tree with a machine-gun.

A crack and a thump as Meretrich falls out of a tree.

A fierce whisper floats out of the sky. 'Mac! Mac!'

'What?' from another disembodied patch of sky.

'How high do you have to go?'

'Hey?'

'I'm ten feet off the ground, is that high enough?'

'What do you think rhinos can do – jump?'

Small is having hysterics. After a while, the baboons hesitantly descend.

'Merry, you can come down now.'

'Fuck off.'

'No, it's all right, it's gone, come down.'

'Fuck off!'

Eventually Meretrich decides not to spend the rest of the night in a tree and comes down, torn and bleeding because it was a thorn tree, comes stumbling, cursing through the snapping jesse.

'Merry, you can't get through there, you'll have to go round.'

'Hey?'

'You can't get through, go round.'

Pause. 'I'm going home.'

In 1978, poaching for rhino horn has scarcely begun, but the threat exists, it is rife across the river in Zambia, and it surfaces in conversation before the night fire.

'What I don't get,' says Lager, 'is that these idiots are just wiping out the source of their own revenue. They don't seem to care that it'll run out one day.'

'They're Afs, mun,' says Meretrich, 'They don't think about tomorrow.'

'Most of the hunters are just poor starving peasants from Zambia, though, give them a gun, pay them a few bucks, they can't resist it . . .'.

'It's the stinking rich government bastards behind it I hate, and those Chinese quacks . . .'.

'They're de*luded*! Rhino horn is just keratin, they might as well chew their fingernails!'

'Ah swear to Gott,' fumes Gdansk, 'anyone comes 'ere to kill ma rhino, I'll tear 'im to pieces with ma bare 'ands.'

Tim cuts in, smooth and quiet. 'You realise that compassion for animals is a cultural thing. And it's mostly just us *mukiwas*, luxury-laden Westerners. It's sentiment, it's ersatz. Killing anything, even other people, means there's been a failure of the imagination, to *be* that animal. That imagining, *that's* true compassion.'

At that moment, Tim Boot reminds me of my mother.

I think about my mother then. All her life, she has invested an apparently unlimited capacity for love – and with it, necessarily, an almost equally unlimited capacity to bear pain – in protecting from human encroachment her patch of the Vumba mountains, that astonishingly rich tract of evergreen forest and montane grassland. Through her hands – frequently bitten, horned and scratched in the process – have passed bushbuck and duiker, mongoose and genet, bushbaby, bushpig, monkey, kitten and bird. No injured orphan is left to die; no creature caged for longer than it takes to rehabilitate it to its natural state. Nothing is fenced; nothing exploited for financial gain: the trees' and animals' freedom to be themselves is solely and completely her passion.

I consider myself extraordinarily, almost magically, lucky to have been raised there. I am lucky to have been released into the world, just like another orphan, unburdened by expectations, and unconditionally loved. Of course, just as she knows that she may be releasing her bushbuck fawn into the jaws of the resident leopard, my mother has been obliged uneasily to release me into the dangerous world of armed and conscience-less men.

At Mana I find echoes of the dank and sun-splashed womb of her forest, which forms for me the *omphalos,* the world-navel, the fountainhead, of all regenerative possibility, compassion, and peace. Mana is another great haven from the ashen valleys in which humanity wages war against itself and against the indigenous creatures.

* * *

'Don't show me poems,' says Tim forcefully. 'Poems are a wank. I'd never show my poems to anyone. Not anyone.'

So I don't. We share other people's poems, though. We mutually approve of this snatch of poetry, from Conway Powers's 'Guide to a Disturbed Planet':

> We are all bowmen in this place.
> The pattern of the birds against the sky
> Our arrows overprint; and then they die.
> But it is also common to our race
> That when the birds fall down we weep.
> Reason's a thing dimly seen in sleep.

Tim Boot and I agree that the world would be better off without most of the people on it. The sporadic pleasure we take in one another's company wars with our distaste for humanity in the mass; despair conflicts with some ineradicable idealism. Despite ourselves, we are fascinated by human foibles. In one obsessively coagulated poem, I lambaste 'Man' for his follies:

> *With horned hands beyond control*
> *He breaks atoms and burns*
> *His air with banging spears and steel stones,*
> *Throttles on his own dust*
> *And shrapnel.*

Just as well Tim doesn't see that one.

We do not feel angelic ourselves. Tim grimly shoots impala and buffalo for meat. Every time he kills he brushes his fingertips through the blood and presses them to his lips. Not in triumph, he says, but in shame and tribute. I note my unease at our own foolish and unnecessary shooting of the odd guineafowl while on patrol:

> *The guineafowl flops*
> *Useless and shot in the river,*
> *Lost to its killer.*

Niggling guilt, helpless fury at poachers' shots and game-driving fires that smoke the hills of the Zambian bank, general disillusionment with my fellow human beings – all come together somehow to drive me into thinking afresh about God. A once-off visitor to Mana is a languid and angular 'Sky-pilot', an itinerant priest. We take a cruel delight in harrying him into confusion on the issue of personal freedom, sending him away with a defeated, 'Yes, well, these things intrigue me.' Nevertheless, the editor of a little Umtali church newsletter manages to inveigle me into writing something for it. The nearest I can get to religion is yet another eulogy to Mana which I call 'God's World'.

Next thing, I receive a letter from The Jeek congratulating me on becoming a Christian. I'm half-amused, half-horrified, like a Puritan who is confident he can't be seduced but has been tricked into entering a brothel. I write in the diary: 'I won't – can't – disillusion him. Christianity is too fine an ideal for that – I wonder how many times, had I been Christian, I would genuinely have thanked the Lord for my safety and saviour.'

I scribble my tangled worries out in nebulous fragments of poetry:

> *As river flows into ocean,*
> *And sea ripens into rain,*
> *And the rain returns*
> *To sow headwaters,*
> *Let my soul flow into love-tides,*
> *Rise to the harvested skies*
> *And fall again as fruit*
> *To seed the streams*

Then find myself asking, 'Why did I write that? Is my Godlessness a facade?'

I cannot answer myself, cannot articulate it properly even to Tim. Tim is too often aloof, authoritarian, contradictory. Nowhere more so than when he allows me to help him in rearing an orphaned impala fawn, a bundle of tawny legs and enormous glossy eyes. Tim folds his own great shanks around her as he nudges the teat of the bottle between her lips, coaxing and cursing her softly in Shona. They bleat to one another, like mother and child.

Then one day, somehow, Humbleman's Staffordshire terrier gets inside the fort fence, hurls himself yowling against the wire of the fawn's pen, she panics, gashes herself terribly across the face, falls away from the redounding wire, a foreleg broken. Tim doesn't say anything. He takes his black revolver from its holster and holds the fawn's muzzle gently in his hand as he shoots her. He gathers the body up. Blood runs across his forearms. He starts walking towards the river. For the first time I feel the opportunity, the necessity, to reach out to this strange and distant man. I grip his elbow lightly as he passes. 'I'm so sorry, Tim.' He stops. He is shaking. I know that what he really wants to do is shoot the dog, maybe even its owner. Then he walks away, and we leave him, knowing he will throw his orphan's body into the great stream of the Zambezi, where the crocs will feed on it briefly, and the even greater stream of the natural world will simply go on.

Or will it? On another day Tim tells me, tight-jawed, of a plan being mooted to dam the Zambezi again, downriver at Mupata Gorge. Mana Pools would vanish. I put what I've learned from Gerard Manley Hopkins under maximum pressure in an extended paean for a wildlife magazine. 'I am in love with a place,' I wail, 'and they want to flood it from the face of the wild.'

I read it to Tim. He nods, and gives me a long, ruminative look. 'Use my typewriter,' he says.

So Tim's graceless bestowing upon me of a sense of unwarranted privilege struggles with a rootless self-disgust disguised as disgust for the rest of humanity. The struggle finds its way into the episodes of a novel I am starting. I begin sending bits of it to The Jeek for critical comment, on the model of Steinbeck's *Journal of a Novel*, in which he recorded by letter the process of writing *East of Eden*. My own novel is an ungainly combination of historical tract and political thriller. It involves an ill-conceived plot on the part of die-hard white Rhodesians to overthrow an emerging black government, an impossibly beautiful heroine, and a medley of characters whose essential features I rigorously draw up even before I've decided what to do with them. I incorporate actual political events as they come to hand in our belatedly-received newspapers, as well as stories of race-fights around the Salisbury night-clubs brought back from time-off by Meretrich and the other city-slickers. I fill swathes of diary with character-sketches, lists of possible episodes, byzantine speculations on what might happen.

I get stuck. I brood, get nowhere. The Jeek never writes. After some weeks, I take what feels like my life in my damp hands. I ask Tim, 'If you won't look at poems, will you look at fiction?' He nods. I read out some bits of it.

He gives me his straight, non-committal look. 'It's one way of cutting your teeth,' he says.

I know I can go no further. I feel its fraudulence, like a nausea. I take the sheets I have written out and, with the aid of the aviation fuel we use to light our boiler-fire, burn them. The flakes drift in blue death up through the branches of the acacias. I feel unaccountably light and satisfied.

* * * * *

Chapter 5

On the Fringes

PARADOXICALLY, in the middle of the vast expanse of the Zambezi Valley, Mana's tiny defensive outpost remains claustrophobic. Even in the middle of its heated intimacy, I often feel lonely, marginalised. Still, I am infinitely happier than I ever was at Llewellin. Living on top of each other breeds the odd squabble, but there is no one I really dislike. Our little community is refreshed by constant shifts. Rangers and NS take staggered R&R.

We are relieved by occasional visitors: Pookie drivers, Parks officials checking up on us, wanderers with no apparent purpose at all. A couple of grimly manic Selous Scouts stagger off under 70-kilo packs into Zambia, presumably to be uplifted somewhere else, since they do not return. There is a vitriolic brute who has been invalided out of SAS, has driven pantechnicons across Canada, is uniformly scathing about blacks, American Indians, and Indian Indians, and has no turn of humour that does not predate on someone else's sensibilities.

The gimlet-eyed provincial warden with his tight helmet of iron-grey hair and an unshakeable, self-effacing smile, one evening forges a memorable conversation which ranges over the capabilities of satellites (the security forces' raid on Chimoio in Mozambique was compromised thus before it even got there), the habits of Australian bullfrogs (some burrow ten feet under sand and can stay there for eighteen years, waiting for rain), the feats and minds of stuntmen and trapeze-artists, and diving in Sinoia Caves (100 feet down it's still so clear you can see pied kingfishers flickering above the surface).

In the absence of such luminaries, evening conversations in the fort are of a rather different order:

A: 'Well, we didn't enjoy the First World War much, but what about Burma '44, hey?'

B: '– the floods were bad, boy!'

A: '– and how did you dig the Congo?'

B: 'That's a bad place, I tell you, I nearly went moggy in that jungle, hey.'

A: 'That's only because you got that bump on the head, when that bus ran over your face.'

B: 'Ja, that was nasty, hey! The bus was *fucked*.'

A: 'It didn't even have the tyres on, just the rims.'

B: 'Ja, well – I was hungry! [Pause] Heavy indigestion after that. That was the day you caught that anaconda, wasn't it?'

A [nodding]: 'Egyptian Spitting Python, actually.'

B: 'Egyptian? In the Congo?'

A: 'Congo Spitting Python, then. Distinctive sound . . . *kgkpsssth-hgyx!*'

One itinerant Pookie driver, a rough-cut farmer from Gatooma, is known as Bulldustin' Boet for his transparently invented 'warries' (war stories). But we think there is more than a grain of truth in Bulldustin' Boet's story of Lassie Wynn. Lassie Wynn is a notorious strip-artist and troopies' delight. I remember seeing an article about her in the *Illustrated Life Rhodesia*, complete with photograph. I angled the page to the light to detect the shadow of a nipple. Lassie can be hired for private gatherings for $70.

'So you see, my wife was away,' relates Boet, mournful sighs broken by hissing nasal laughter and clucks of anger. 'Me and my mates from the farms there, y'know, we were *horny*, ay. So we think, h-yell, seventy clams isn't much between us, we'll get her in. So she rocks up with this weedy oke, bloody pimp, reckons he's her husband, I dunno. Anyway, there she's in my own lounge, strips off, spec-fucking-tacular, she hangs her panties on my wife's favourite vase, ay!'

'So she gets right down with you?'

'Hey, it's all hands off, ay, the pimp is right there, but she shoves her tits in my face, *C'mon farmer, give 'em a good suck.* Whew! H-yell! Well, next thing I know this bloody pimp is there saying, You don't give me five hundred bucks I'm gonna tell your wife about this.' Boet mops his brick-red forehead and moans, 'I've already been divorced twice, man, I can't afford another one. So I paid, ay.'

The most frequent Pookie-pilot is Archie, our bleached-out Archbishop Makarios look-alike, with his long yellow beard and yellowing teeth. He is quiet and unobtrusively kind. He once detects a landmine only 50 metres out of camp. We think, Christ, these bastards are getting bold all of a sudden. Archie gingerly digs it up, a battered-looking TM57. It is empty of explosive and it has a note taped to the top of it: 'That should wake you up, Archie!' Tim and Gdansk's idea of a joke.

Two weeks later we learn that Archie has been killed in an ambush somewhere, the Pookie disabled, he was gunned down as he tried to climb out of that terrible funnel of a cab.

For a time we are joined by the graders and bulldozers of a Roads Department contingent, come in to repair the washaways and refurbish the roads. They establish themselves at the old South African Police camp a few hundred metres upstream. (There are numerous derogatory tales told about the South African Police: how, for instance, going out on patrol, the gunner would cradle his MAG under a rain cape, barrel sticking out one side, butt the other – and nothing in between – working parts being far too heavy to lug all over the shateen.) The Roads people are guarded by a raffish and voluble contingent of Rhodesia Defence Regiment 'goffles'. The name, they laughingly explain, is derived from 'God's own forgotten lost souls'. They are Coloured territorials; they are not noticeably burdened by their reputation for grotesque inefficiency and slaphappy irresponsibility. Some of them occasionally wander over to beg Tim to shoot an impala and to entertain us with the vivacity of their distinctive patois:

'Ay, china, I scheme we should take a dip in the Zam, I'm melting like a vanilla in Hell, ay!'

'Nooit, china, the fladdog'll have you for teatime, ek sê, those blerry lizards are r-r-ravenous, jong!'

'Ag, no, we just goof with our gats, mun!'

'Nooit, Ah don't smaak this place, ay, gimme ol' Skies back.'

'Oh, yeh, Bula-way-over-there!'

'Coke an' buns, ja!'

'Bump an' graaaind, ek sê!'

'Ohhh, yussus, jus' to put some motion-lotion in my ol' social vroom, and when the lights tune favour, I drop rubber, an' evaporate here and an' condense over theeeere, ek sê!'

When the time comes for this lot to go home, the Pookie is unavailable, but they are going anyway, with one soldier perched gaily on their Four-Five's roll-bar.

'Ay, china, you better strap in, what happens to you if you hit a road-bomb, ay?'

'Ag well, Ah tune Ah'll be the first goffle to hit the *moon*, ek sê!'

* * *

We all, every two or three weeks, disappear for days into the impenetrable jesse, those featureless regions of low tangled scrub, mostly spiny sickle-bush and similar thorny horrors, all that will grow on that poor Kalahari sand.

Patrols are both the main activity and the main safety valve. I find them an increasingly attractive escape from the wearying days of radio-watch. Some of us even begin to request them. We feel personally insulted if refused.

9 Sept. There are a couple of Army sticks in the Rukomeche area, so we decide to go Sapi way instead, inland where we went with the Old NS.

We (myself, Laptop and Meretrich) with game scouts Anodi and Josiah, leave Mana 7.45, cutting onto the airfield road and then the Old Security Road.

Mana floodplain: 2 buffalo, 6 zebra, 5 warthog, 1 waterbuck, 4 impala.

Mopane: ± 40 buffalo, some lion growling but unseen, heralded by some birds making a 'chirrr' sound – this might also indicate rhino. Another word for lion is 'mondhoro'.

Rest at Old Security Road 0900.

Chiruwe River 1000. Turn south for 3 km to water along heavy track. Lunch.

We've discovered that we've forgotten one of the most important items for a patrol – matches – with only 1/4' of fuel left in M's lighter. If it doesn't last out we'll just have to rub the game scouts together.

The pan is a muddy one. One jumbo, and the usual squealing baboons. Hot as Hades, and we lie and wait for the cool.

Leave Chiruwe 1500; bash east through a jesse strip into mopani, shortly a pan, 1 spotted hyena. Thence mostly mopani with patches of jesse and msasa-type grassland. 6 kudu (noro), 2 warthog, 4 impala. Hit a pan 1715; brief supper. Covered approx. 17 km so far, ± 2–3 tonight. Tomorrow we'll cut through to the Zambezi . . .

Most patrols are sleepily beautiful, boyishly indulgent. Some turn turbulent with personality clashes. Bullock and Wastrell come to blows over who is to carry the bully-beef. Attempts by stick leaders to instil the discipline normally incumbent on a warrior caste (let alone the safety procedures normal to preserving your skin in a guerrilla war) are frequently greeted with derision and surly rebelliousness. We seldom 'push guard'. OPs are compromised by shooting up stray log dugouts with the MAG or, more often, by a display of naked buttocks somersaulting into the river. It's a miracle none of us is noshed by a croc.

But now and then we are reminded that, even in this rough Eden, we exist on the margins of a greater war. The Pookie does pick up the odd landmine on the road. One of them is all buckled on one side, it has been run over so often; why it hasn't been detected before is a mystery. Another has seven slabs of TNT packed underneath it. Neither has been primed to detonate.

'Jeez, they're a bunch of incompetents!'

'Just as well, think what woulda happened, ay . . .'.

There are other signs, too: a hammer-and-sickle carved into a baobab tree, the muddied label of a Tanzanian bully-beef tin, an AK doppie, a dugout pulled up onto the sand, Marz boot tracks which I carefully sketch. There are shots on the far side of the river. Some of these are certainly hunters, we can hear the elephant panicking. But we also know that out here in the lawless wilderness there is no clear distinction between hunters and soldiers. We seem more likely, though, to be shot by Rhodesian Army sticks straying unannounced across the Rukomeche River.

Only once in these six or seven months do we really get a fright. We are conducting one of our usual ridiculous OPs on the river-bank somewhere, we hear shots on the far side. One is unusually flat, like a shotgun. We have seen nothing and worry less. Moving into gonk posi at nightfall, we have trouble finding a suitable spot, and rather arbitrarily execute a wide dog-leg before bedding down in an unimpressive grove of mopane scrub. During the night we suddenly find ourselves in wakeful rigidity, listening to the sound of footsteps crunching by through the dry leaves. I dare not even lift a hand to my rifle.

The footsteps fade; we push guard for the rest of the night. At dawn we scout about; there are tracks everywhere, a place where three dugouts were pulled up the bank and launched again, a freshly-dropped bakelite AKM magazine, heavy with rounds. There is no question that twelve or fifteen guerrillas came across after dark and split into pairs to look for us.

We set up another, slightly more careful OP. We see nothing. But late in the afternoon we hear that same flat report from over the river, suddenly wonder if it is some kind of signal that we've been spotted again. We hightail out of there like panicked impala.

The fright is all but forgotten on our return. Exciting news: Gdansk, who has been off in Wankie National Park on an elephant cull, has been injured. A wounded elephant got him, tossed him in the air, ripped his scrotum open on a scything tusk. Tim seems to think it's hilarious, gets me to draw a get-well cartoon: Gdansk impaled on the end of an elephant tusk like a marshmallow on a toothpick.

When Gdansk gets back, mincing a little but otherwise full of the survivor's exaggerated spunk, Tim and I stage a pantomime of the whole thing. The fort reverberates in a brief storm of laughter.

Tim suddenly collapses into gloom, slumps in his chair with his long hands thrust between his knees. His eyes are glazed china, as if he has had a premonition, or seen the Void.

'He's brooding on his woman again,' whispers Meretrich.

'Meaning?'

'Didn't you know? Apparently his girlfriend was culled in an ambush near Selous a couple of years ago. Never gotten over it.'

'Oh,' whispers Wastrell, 'I thought it was his *sister*.'

'It was his *chick*, mun. She was preggers.'

But Tim never speaks of it. I never will find out if it is true.

* * *

We are on the fringes in many ways. As New NS we are disdained by the Old NS; as NS, disdained by the rangers; as 'Zookeepers', marginalised by the Army. War is being waged, but for us only by report, scraps of news coming in like sinister, momentary moths flickering in our beam of mellow Zambezi light.

24 June. At 9 P.M. last night terrorists hacked to death thirteen missionaries in Elim Mission just a few k's from my folks' place! – two men, three women, seven girls and a nine-month-old baby. No doubt there will be the usual useless outcries, the usual reversal of charges onto Selous Scouts. The fact that the victims were British may have some effect somewhere, but I doubt it. People are curiously fond of ignoring brutality when it doesn't directly affect them. I don't want to live in a country with people capable of such barbarities – perhaps I don't want to live with humanity.

25 June. We had a long discussion last night on the future of the country and the educational system. We're all generally agreed that Rhodesia's had it.

10 August. One of the goffle contingents has been ambushed near Rukomeche Research Station; something like four injuries.

31 August. 10.30 Radio announcement; the President Hon. J.J. Wrathall, died early this morning. There are rumours that he committed suicide, or was murdered, after cottoning onto some illegal government deal concerning G3 rifles.

The story goes that the Army is pulling out, becoming totally mobile, and whenever there's a scene they'll rush in anything up to 6 companies to sort them out. Assuming it's true, the system has its advantages and disadvantages . . .

It seems the Security Forces are at a loss as to how to continue, if they are prepared to undergo a complete reversal of tactics. Perhaps they're simply preparing for the big scene, unbeknown to the general public: according to Gdansk, the regulars are all being revamped in their 'digging-in' techniques.

While the Army pull out, doubtless we'll be left out on a limb as usual. Yesterday they changed the radio frequency again without informing us, and Bullock had fun and games trying to reestablish comms. From all angles a sorry scene.

5 Sept. *The past three days have been characterised by speculation, and horror, over the disappearance of an Air Rhodesia Viscount five minutes out of Kariba, Salisbury-bound. It has transpired that eight people out of the fifty-two passengers and four crew have survived. Eighteen survived the crash itself; ten injured were murdered by terrorists who initially claimed to have come to help, including a four-year-old girl . . . It suddenly occurred to me that the Scripture Union Kariba camp, B [The Jeek's sister], TB et al went on, flew up, and might have been flying back . . .*

The old political situation is slowly collapsing, with Smith's 'secret' meeting with Joshua Nkomo and other ZAPU heavies. Apparently it was Nkomo who insisted the meeting be kept secret, but it was Nkomo who revealed it; looks like he's conned Smith into something.

7 Sept. *It has been established that the Viscount was brought down by a heat-seeking missile. A long-planned attack, obviously, a well-equipped group, and I wouldn't be surprised if it's the same group that hit the convoy at Rhodes and Founders. Bastards.*

A bounty has been placed on the heads of Nkomo and Mugabe; an offer of $100 000 to bring them to trial. Even 'irregular justice' is acceptable, according to the Minister of Law and Order.

Smith says he is initiating a 'new policy' in Rhodesia's defence; I wonder if he's had a card up his sleeve or if he's just beating around for a way out.

8 Sept. *Umtali got revved last night; two people slightly injured, a good deal of damage.*

13 Sept. *The papers give a full list of the passengers on the downed Viscount. No one I knew.*

14 Sept. *Very bad vehicle accident on the Zambezi escarpment road, 6 or 7 injured, one dead: Starlight [medic] . . . sounds horribly like my old friend from Llewellin, Brinjal. I can't get the picture of his long sad face out of my mind . . . Can't be sure yet, though.*

15 Sept. Wastrel comes back from Marongora, and confirms it was Brinjal who was killed. The drunken bastard of a driver naturally got away with it. Sickening. Apparently going around an S-bend on the escarpment, the truck hit the cliff-side, the driver over-corrected as they went off the other edge, the truck flipped so that it came down back first, only being held from going further down the slope by the crash-cables. B had an arm sheared off by a cable and a rib driven into his heart. I go off and brood along the river-bank. I keep thinking of Brinje and me standing in the rain staring at our boots that time. Tim senses my distress, asks me. Now it's his turn to squeeze my elbow and say how sorry he is.

16 Sept. The news this morning says the Security Forces have had the most successful killing fortnight since December 1972, with 165 terrs killed, 33 collaborators and 6 recruits. A loss of 11.

23 Sept. Rhodesia's latest incursion into Mozambique is in its third day.

25 Sept. Disturbing news: nearly a fifth of the country has been placed under martial law. The declaration of martial law is the step immediately bordering on anarchy.

26 Sept. Smith has chaired his last Parliament meeting before his retirement from politics. Another white bastion gone.

16 Oct. Evening [on patrol]. Report 4–5 shots 'probably across the river', and almost inadvertently discover that there's a heavy contact going on, and a follow-up of 7–9 CTs, possibly two wounded, involving 24F and 23A. Our scant lists have now been emended to conform with the Army's, so we are able to ascertain that their position is about 30 k's south of us, heading north, around the escarpment somewhere probably. Anyway, everybody's taking our report very seriously and giving us all sorts of suggestions for sweeps, ambushes and OPs.
   We go to bed.

19 Oct. Our last full day out on this patrol . . . 24D, an Army stick, is at Mana main camp, talking about drums of fuel. The reason becomes evident later, as we move down to the river just upstream of Mucheni. At around nine, Alouette helicopters are heard churning, and a heavy-pistoned job that must be a Dakota. Sikanda spots four choppers hopping over the mountains into Zambia. Then the jets – four Canberras and three Hunters – sweep low over the river, up over the Zambian escarpment, turn west. Wild excitement over this evidently quite big 'external'. 0945 and the four choppers skip back into Mana . . .

We join the crocs for a splash.

1100. The Alouettes go back into Zambia, almost lost in the haze.

1115. Two, perhaps three, Lynxes cross, to our west this time, the other side of Vundu hill.

1130. More jets, this time too high to be seen, and very fast. Mirages?

1300. The Lynxes come back home.

1500. The Lynxes go back into Zambia. A little later the Canberras and Hunters, evidently having returned to refuel and rearm by a different route, pass almost overhead back to the strike area. The heart thrills to hear the multiple snarl and growl of the Lynxes and Canberras' great rumble and the Hunters' whistle and hiss. The choppers have been batting about all afternoon . . .

The two black game scouts are not impressed with all these goings-on. Bullock and Wastrell deride them as 'gutless' and 'all the same' – but I can't blame them for having some affinity with their black brethren across the river. White must be a common enemy. Especially when Wastrell says stupid and indefensible things like 'lekker!' [nice!] when they question the bombing of civilians.

20 Oct. Back at Mana (0715), we hear the full story of the raids. Three camps have been hit . . .

An estimated 450 were killed in the Lusaka camp, 500+ in the SAS-hit one, and none in the RLI's, which turned out to be empty . . . According to Nkomo, 226 were killed and some 600 injured, 190 having been immediately discharged. Nkomo claims that the camp was not his headquarters as the Rhodesians alleged, that it housed civilians involved in market gardening and maize-growing. Evidently the fat slug's very angry and threatening retaliatory raids, and we can

fully expect attacks here, too. Nkomo also disclaims Rhodesian state-
ments, to the effect that the Zambians were forewarned of the attack
in order that civilians could be withdrawn, as propaganda – which is
probably true . . .

I hear the enemy had a 12.7mm cannon mounted on the other
side which was causing a bit of trouble, and either it or another one
damaged a Dakota. Evidently it has been taken out since, as the chop-
pers are still thrashing back and forth low over the trees.

And in the middle of all this frenetic, roaring aerial activity,
Wastrell's high voice goes floating over the air to the road camp up-
stream: 'Do you guys want a game of volleyball?'

21 Oct. I hear we lost one helicopter, crashed, injuries only. Perhaps
that heavy explosion we heard while at Mucheni was them destroying
the wreck.

29 Oct. The word from a friend of Tim's who works at St Giles' re-
habilitation centre, is that the pilot of the helicopter that crashed in
Zambia is now a vegetable.

So we watch from our waterside exile as the war churns around us.
Paradoxically, the violence comes closest to us on the one occasion
we get out of Mana on a shopping trip. We have to walk all the way
out, some 70 k's in a day and a bit, get blistered feet, nearly tread on
lions, get scuffled out of our sleeping-bags again by an inquisitive
rhino. For a long time the blue rim of the escarpment seems to recede
ahead of us, then is lost behind thick mopane, and finally reappears,
a miraculous wave, looming heavily above us.

In the afternoon we book ourselves into the ducal rooms of the
Makuti Motel, stuff ourselves with steak, egg and chips. It is the
Rhodes and Founders long weekend (Rogues and Scroungers, collo-
quially), the atmosphere is celebratory. I do not join the boozy revelry
of the others in the bar, but retire alone to our room to read and doze
in the reddening evening light.

But that is only the beginning of the evening.

Later, I will write it all up as a kind of short story.

* * *

'Dan, open the door, quickly, for Chrissake, Danny!'

Laptop, desperate. Slapped the book down, long strides, swung the hotel room door open. Laptop standing there, camouflage shirt torn open, Dutch-chubby face red and panting, sweat-streaked. Florid hand white on the heavy MAG's carrying-handle, shoulders draped with the clinking tresses of rounds, all we'd brought, uncoiling pythons of brass over his plastered forearm.

'Jesus, what's up, Irv? Come in, man!'

'Just get me a glass of water, for God's sake, get me some water.' I hauled off some of the ammo belts as he staggered in, headed for the adjoining bathroom. No glass. 'Damn,' aloud. What the hell's wrong with this motel?

'Here's one.' Laptop on his knees by the big bed, he handed me the glass from the pokey dresser, clumsy. I filled it quickly, and he slurped mouthfuls noisily. I helped him drag himself wearily onto the bed, and he collapsed there, rubbing his good hand across his forehead.

'Okay, just take it easy, Irv, just relax.'

Laptop grunted, moaned, turned his head slowly from side to side, pinched his eyes.

'My God, Jesus God . . .'.

'Easy, Irv. What happened, mate?'

'There's been an accident. Bull and Merry've been casevacked.'

'Jesus, no!'

Laptop's voice was short-breathed, loud, the words came tumbling out, the skin white around the working mouth, flushed head framed in the scuffed unruly hair.

'I swear, Dan, it was bad, hey! There's been a fucking ambush, just up the drag here, three dead, ten injured.' He paused, swallowed.

'They hit the convoy?' I could feel the horror building up inside me.

'Ja, they hit the bus, ripped the shit out of it. And we heard, we were in the bar, boozing it up, hey. Oh God Danny, pinting it there, and we were all excited, with all the grog, and as soon as we heard, it was all, Let's go let's go, let's go and kill the bastards, you know?'

Yes, alone, reading in the cosy motel room, I'd heard their singing, had heard the truck, had heard Meretrich hooting wildly, and wondered, half-resentful, where they were going without me.

'Ah God, Dan, I swear, I'm never going to touch drink again, I swear it, never again. Never!' He was talking loudly, too loudly. Mild shock, I stilled him. He drank a little more water, continued more calmly.

'Anyway, me and Merry and Bully jumped on the Two-Five. This driver said, D'you want to come, so of course we were excited, all – you know, jumpy, so we tuned Ja, and us and the driver – his name was Simon or something – and Chunky – you know Chunky, that short little guy we saw this morning and said he looked like Abie's brother – well, he *is* Abie's brother, ja, Chunky and another Army guy. Oh ja, and there was this other cat – he was a good bugger, hey, he kept saying to the driver, Listen cool it, just slow down, because that tit was going so fast. I swear, Danny, Jeez I was scared, I was so shit-scared I moved right under the roll-bar, you know that roll-bar, because I knew, I just knew, sure as fate, that cunt was going to prang it. Oh God . . .'.

And he trailed away again, wiped his wrist across his eyes, shifting painfully on the bed. I told him to relax again, he was getting worked up, the gestures of his good hand too emphatic, the eyes too feverish-bright. Sure as fate. And something, some quirk of chance, had dictated that I shouldn't have been there, that they shouldn't have come to call me. It was the sensible ones who escaped, I told myself.

'I swear it, Dan, I'm going to be like you, I'm never going to drink again, never touch a drop, I swear it . . . That driver, hey, Jesus Dan, we dropped that good guy off at the cop shop, then we came back to fetch a tracker – someone said the tracker was up in the bar – so we came – and going round those corners, oh my God . . .'.

And I could imagine it, too, that fast Two-Five swaying its stubby hips across the road on its big wheels and its soft bouncy springs.

'We came up here, and I was going to get off, because I was so scared, shit I was frightened, Dan – maybe I shouldn't have gone in the first place, because of my arm' – and he lifted the off-white plaster, legacy of a fall a week before – 'but hell, I wanted to help, I thought I could do something, anything. But anyway, I was going to get off when we got back up here to the motel, but oh God, the next thing I knew we were off again – the tracker was down in the compound – and we went screaming down the hill, you know the steep hill at the back here, the exit, and Jesus, Danny, you know that bastard was accelerating down that hill, forget braking, hey! He was just going too fast to bloody turn, you just can't turn at that speed. Now I was sitting facing backwards, okay, under that roll-bar, and I had my back to the generator – they had this bloody great generator in the back, and if it hadn't been tied down, Jesus, I dunno – anyway, I was facing back like this, hey, so I didn't see fuck-all, and the first thing I knew we'd hit something – and I just thought, I knew it, I knew it – and there was this civvy truck standing at the petrol pumps – you know those petrol pumps at the bottom of the hill, and you have to drive round them to get onto the main road? – an RMS truck, and there were these two okes in the cab, and all I saw was the door peeling away and this body flying through the air, Jesus God . . .'.

Again he paused, breathless, laying his eyes into the crook of his arm, mumbling that his hip was hurting. He slurped at some more water, asked for something to eat; there was some biltong in Meretrich's pack, and he tore and sucked at it hungrily.

'And you know, Danny, we creamed that civvy truck so hard that it turned right around – we hit the front, as it was facing this way, okay, to the left, and we knocked it right round so that it was facing to the right, hey! We were shunting, I tell you, Dan. Then the next thing I knew we were over that embankment, you know the one along the main drag, all bloody ten feet of it. And Jesus, we were lucky, we were going so fast, hey, that we went like this' – and he demonstrated with the plane of his hand how the front wheels had hit the edge of the road and the back had come down. He rolled his head, and the movement passed sluggishly down into his body.

'You know, Dan, if we'd been going any slower, or if we'd hit that bank sideways, we wouldn't have ramped like that, we'd have flipped, we'd have been culled. I swear, someone up there was looking after us today, oh boy. But even so, Jesus! We were lucky we were a bit drunk, hey, because we were all relaxed, you know – hell, you know old Chunky? Old Chunky was right at the back of the truck, hey, and he flew right over the front and landed on the island on the other side of the road, on the concrete. And he was all right! I reckon if he hadn't been so pissed he would have been stuffed.'

'As it was, Chunky and I were the only two to get out all right,

Bullock's shoulder's messed, Merry's bust both his feet – I don't know how he did it but – ay, and the driver's stuffed, hey – broken back.'

Inside me a little tightening of horror, revulsion, something, but I knew I agreed with Laptop when he said: 'But I've got no sympathy with him, Dan, no sympathy at all. He could have killed me, he could have wiped us all out – and – I'm sorry, but I'm too young to die because of some drunken arsehole. I don't give a fuck – uh-uh, no, never again, never!'

He was silent for a while then, the gesticulating hand resting on the plastered one, eyes closed. I looked out the wide window between the deep curtains, down the hill and across the crinkled valleys and stippled green trees fading into blue, late sunlight pouring molten across the far silver streak of the edge of the lake. A beautiful world, I thought, then I looked at Laptop's puffy face, thought of broken ankles and flying bodies and screaming wheels and thought again, What a beautiful world for such terrible things to happen in.

'And the MAG's bust as well,' Laptop said, low in his throat, 'just check it for me, Dan, please.'

For the moment, the health of the weapon was more important than his own body.

'You better go and get hold of the rangers at Marongora, Dan, tell them. I'll have a hot bath, see if I can ease this hip a bit.'

When I got back from the phone Laptop was still lying on the bed.

'There's no hot water, Dan.'

'Ah shit!'

A servant came round then, carrying clean sheets; the electricity had gone, he said. No lights; another minor disaster, we felt.

There was a sudden flurry of traffic up the hill to the motel, and suddenly I remembered the ambush, the greater calamity to which Laptop's accident had been a mere sideshow. Laptop cocked his head, raised a finger, hoisting himself slowly upright.

'That'll be the back half of the convoy,' he said, 'they sent them back.'

We pushed the MAG under the bed, locked the door, and walked slowly up to the motel itself, Laptop limping, stiff-backed. The people off the convoy were going in, pale, chattering. Bullock was there, stained T-shirt, floppy hat, one arm in an ostentatious sling, walking too quickly, speaking too quickly, somewhere between nervous and showing off. He'd gone down to the airfield with the ambush victims, he said: a seventeen-year-old girl had died there, head wound. Four dead. He complained of his shoulder, shook his head. 'Hmmm-m. Back to the bar for me, boy!' Laptop and I looked at each other. Bullock walked quickly away as though on an important errand.

Laptop and I went in, sat in the slumped couch in the brown-hued lounge, listening to the shocked and vibrant stories sobbing around us. There were a lot of people there, food ran out quickly, daylight quicker, and the people became as subdued as the candle-light flaking and rippling on the walls, so quiet you could hear the spit and flap of the fireplace flames. I watched the candle's vacillating bulb flickering in soft ranks down the grainy chair-arms, watched how it made Laptop's eyes sag into tired and melancholy pools. We sat there for a long time, sipped coffee and Coke, until they started singing, raucous and ragged, in that other world in the bar. Laptop stirred himself then, we rose, and he was shaking his head slowly as we went out into the night.

* * *

Only towards the end of the year does it become clear that none of us will be allowed to stay on at Mana Pools, as I have been fervently hoping. This adds to my habitual gloom about the world 'out there'. On that most hallowed memorial of Rhodesian self-importance, 11 November, I write:

Independence Day today: fourteen years of struggle and survival. I can't see it making fifteen, any way it works, even though Smith is adamant the transition will not take place before the end of the year. While the martial law areas and external raids may be helping militarily, as General Walls claims (probably propaganda!), the same raids are alienating the overseas powers whose co-operation seems essential to the survival of a democratic Rhodesia. Thus the British Parliament overwhelmingly votes for the reimposition of sanctions, the all-party conference (which may or may not help) hovers on a receding horizon, the country limps on. The Executive Committee comes to odds, and so does everybody else. The same factionalism, selfishness, power-hunger, that have ever, and ever will, plague mankind.

I turn back to recording the movements of rhino, the textures of sandbanks, the return of Kleinkie, one of our tame warthogs, missing for four days and reeking, I suspect, of requited sex.

One brassy and stifling November morning, Tim calls.

'Bullock. Dan. Escort out to the airstrip, ndegi coming in.'

We rattle out there to clear the dusty strip of elephants and herons, as a glistening Cessna drifts in like a winged promise.

Tim hoists a fat backpack from the Land-Rover.

'Where are you going?'

'Long leave,' he grins. 'I probably won't see you lot again. Ever. Cheers.'

And he folds his long limbs into the plane like a pocket-knife, and leaves us gaping in a snarling swirl of indifferent dust.

'Well, good riddance,' spits Bullock. 'Arsehole.'

I feel betrayed, bereft, stung. No warning. Not a handshake. Not a word for the future. Perhaps there was, after all, no narrative.

Tim is temporarily replaced by a swarthy, manic individual named Tenniel. He is so improbably narrow-faced, his ruler-straight blade of a nose defended by close-set eyes uncompromising as agate, that he is immediately dubbed Werewolf. Werewolf is absurdly young, insanely energetic. He claims to have been a US Navy Seal. He *rocketed* up through National Parks' ranks, he says.

'Well, that's not so difficult if you are white and a good shot,' growls Lager under his breath.

Werewolf institutes a regimen of frenetic efficiency. A practice shoot on the little range reveals that half the weapons in the fort jam through inattention, and we spend a day in the broiling summer sun polishing every one of thousands of MAG rounds. He stages a mock night attack with thunderflashes; none of the game-scouts are in the know, Werewolf and Gdansk convincingly run from turret to turret, checking and exhorting. Husky with bridled fear, Anodi whispers, 'If they come through those trees I will pour fires of hot lead into them!' Then Werewolf shepherds them into C turret and gets them singing, deep surging melodies with whistling and keening counterpoint. Werewolf shouts, 'Who is dada?' And they bellow in unison,

'Baas Tenniro!' and 'Mana Number One! Fockoff gandangas! Fock-off coke-and-buns Marongora!'

Yet through all Werewolf's conversations a devilish racism glints cruelly; he relishes the tales of black-white violence Bullock and others bring back from Salisbury's night-streets, encouraging the re-tellings with barely restrained stabs of his brown fists.

When out on a day-walk with Wastrell, he sees floating down the river what Wastrell is certain is the remnant of a baobab tree. Werewolf insists it's a dugout with two terrorists crouching in it. Wastrell has fun anyway revving the offending object with MAG fire. It sails serenely on. When some RDR men slouch over the fol-lowing day, the number of terrs in the 'canoe', in Werewolf's excited retelling, has blossomed to six. Four bodies have been collected by helicopter!

He begins to see gooks behind every sickle-bush. When out fish-ing on the nearest island with Bullock and me one day he suddenly stiffens and says, 'There's somebody on the other side!'

Indeed, elephant are running, trumpeting. The far bank maybe seven hundred metres off.

'There's someone watching, under that big tree. I can see him! Don't look at him, just me look, you look somewhere else.'

We look at the ground and at the sky.

'Shall I shoot him?' chatters Werewolf.

Bullock enthuses, his irony lost on Werewolf, 'Ja, pull 'im, Tenn!'

'But he'll see me aiming and run away.'

'Come behind these bushes, then.'

'Ag, I don't want to just injure him,' objects Werewolf, 'or miss him. I've got to kill 'im, straight. I need scopes. Agh, he's gone!'

We skirmish back across the all but naked island.

Come evening, Werewolf says, 'They were setting up mortars, I'm sure of it. I'm telling you, we're going to get revved tonight. We'll get mortared at half-past-six.'

'But Tenn, it's already twenty to seven.'

'Well, half-past-seven, then.'

We miss keenly Tim's sanity, even his stiff gloom.

In the closing days of late December, Werewolf keeps us on tenterhooks over when and whether we are finally to leave. He makes no secret of the fact he'll be glad to see the last of us. 'Fuckin' wankers'. We have little to do beyond slashing the fort lawn and devouring books. Some newspapers come in. I glumly summarise:

> *Splits are evident everywhere, on both black and white sides. The Transitional Government appears to have mended its discord over the postponement of elections, but will this split the Government from the people? . . .*
>
> *Comrade Max's 'safe areas' are now areas in which terrorists have taken over and 'liberated' from 'weak-willed' Security Forces. Meanwhile Nkomo has again rejected an all-party conference; and Britain and the US will continue to pander to him. Senator McGovern, out from the States, says Smith isn't doing enough towards the transition. It remains to be seen what happens when the Land Tenure Act is repealed, as it is due to be on the 19th of December. I'll not be surprised at unprecedented violence.*

When the time finally comes for us to load up onto our final convoy out of Mana, hurt and loss press like a sullen glacier behind my eyes and tweak at the corner of my mouth. Passing through the unbelievable green of the summer jesse, I try to recall some of the ordinary, extraordinary things with which our days have been filled. The scarlet dragonflies, the porcelain blue-green depth of a dead impala's eye. The names of the little tame warthogs: Oortjies (Little-ears), Kleinkie, and Boozi Butler. Bullock's complex dustbin trap for the hyena that kept raiding the kitchen. The day Wastrell threw a buckshee grenade in the river and killed a fish with its muffled thump. The day we threw Meretrich in the river, the current dragged a sock off: Happy Birthday! The taste of freshly-caught, smoked tigerfish. The spine-thrilling, silvery cry of the fish-eagles. The jarring ubiquity of Radio Five: Jerry Rafferty's 'Baker Street' will be forever incongruously associated with the olive undertow of the Zambezi. The amusing shape of a Zambian hill we call Tit Gomo, the smell of thatch, the creaking canvas chairs of the NS Quarters. The blaze of the Carmine bee-eater colony, the toppies that pecked bread-crumbs from the kitchen table and flitted without dislodging a feather through the chicken-wire mesh, the glossy starlings that tamely strutted the lawns. The creamy weight of our own bread.

And then it is all behind us, gouts of dark blue cloud-shadow flattening the Zambezi Valley's greens as we climb away up the escarpment, glinting through it all the mercurial, vanishing artery of the river.

* * * * *

PART 3

Into the Whirlwind

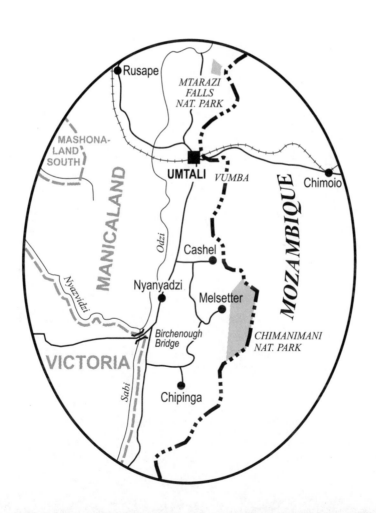

Chapter 6

Pillage and Burn

THREE DAYS before Christmas 1978, the 'tracking course' over, my father picks me up in Salisbury and drives me home. Between the capital and the eastern border, the hills ruckle and bunch in gathering excitement. Isolated, rubicund koppies, bustling like questing moles from the highveld's rolling flats, give way to the whaleback batholiths and granite fins of Rusape and Inyazura, and finally to the maternal, wooded ridges of Umtali Heights, turbulent and worn.

Our Peugeot lunges over the neck of Christmas Pass: Umtali spreads below in a quiet riot of green and scarlet flamboyant-trees, white buildings brilliant as a Greek village in late afternoon sun. The pass curls around the blunt volcanic statements of Murahwa's and Hospital Hills. The arrogant pimple of Cross Koppie, topped by an extravagant stone cross in remembrance of the dead of the 1914–18 war, guards the town's eastern rim. On the far horizon, the hulking ridge of Zohwe and the rounded pyramid of Chinziwa (Standing-at-the-Boundary) mark the beginnings of the Vumba, and of home.

My mother hugs me tightly; the dogs whirl in furry welcome. I look out again across the valley, my vision sharpened with mingled familiarity and strangeness. Umtali is visible across the ridges, a scantling of quartzite chips. In the foreground, the tree-encrusted fin of Nyarusengeri (Place-of-Bamboos) still hunts through rags of effervescent summer cloud. That peak marks the boundary with Mozambique. Its lower slopes are now raked with the russet incisions of a 'Security Road' and the faint fenceline of a minefield. I remember, before 1974, when the Portuguese still held Mozambique and I was an excitable kid, travelling along the road to the coast, just visible from here on the valley floor. In the sensuous humidity of Beira's oil-flecked, jelly-fish-haunted beaches, we bodysurfed, lazed, burned in the sun, jousted warily through the rusted superstructures of The Wreck, and grumbled with angry fascination at the lurking shapes of British destroyers blockading Rhodesia's oil-supplies. They looked wondrously dangerous but were, we were smugly assured, ineffectual.

Mozambique is now the guerrillas' prime base. The eastern border is the most dangerous region in the country. It doesn't look it. In the morning, I settle behind my familiar desk, gaze out of my bedroom window, and write:

> *The day dawns grey-blue and white-misted, the sun flushing the floor of the valley while the dark mountains bury their hunting heads in the cloud. Why should the enemy have that beautiful valley, Mozambique? That is jealousy, and if I were powerful and evil I would invade and take and hold that valley.*

A robust pimple of a koppie is visible on the far side of the valley: Chua Hill. I recall my history teacher telling us the story. In 1891, Colonel Melville Hayman, one of Cecil Rhodes's henchmen, sent a far more substantial force of Portuguese packing: he sat on Chua Hill, fought off an attack, and lobbed a 7-pounder shell into the inflammable rafters of their fort at Macequese. The Portuguese gapped it. Hayman sent his lieutenant, E.W. Fiennes, with 42 men, east to annex the coast. The *whole* coast. It was probably the earliest 'external' by Rhodesian forces. Fiennes got no further than Chimoio, scene of the 1977 Security Forces raid: he was deflected from his act of international banditry by the incoming Bishop of Mashonaland, Dr Knight-Bruce. So 'unfortunately', as the early settler Hans Sauer put it, 'the opportunity of acquiring a very fine and much-needed seaport was lost to Southern Rhodesia'.

I have just acquired Sauer's book, *Ex Africa*, first published in 1937 and now reprinted as part of a series of settler memoirs by a Bulawayo firm, Books of Rhodesia. The series is an invaluable resource for historians, I tell myself; I am interested in becoming an historian. But it is more: to subscribe feels like a mild act of patriotism. One can find there unlimited justification for current attitudes. I open the volume, and read Hans Sauer's account of the legendary ruins of Zimbabwe:

These have remained an unsolved puzzle to archaeologists up to the present, and a great deal of nonsense has been written and conjectured about them. In my opinion they are due, if not to actual construction by the Phoenicians, at least to partly Phoenician influence. The idea that they were built by the African negroid or Bantu races is preposterous, as these races never built anything but huts of straw and sticks . . . Their incapacity to advance is undoubtedly due to the fact, established by De Quatrefages, the great French biologist, that the African races have three and a half ounces of brain matter less than the European.

I remember a neighbour, a stiffly eloquent fruit farmer, passionately arguing exactly this. I am beginning to think that it's simplistic claptrap. But it has become part of our identity, a crucial component of that 'civilisation' in defence of which Ian Smith says he declared UDI in 1965. Tim Boot said to me once, quoting the fantasy writer Ursula le Guin, that the opposite of civilisation is not primitiveness, but war.

A quiver of apprehension hovers sickly behind my sternum. It is not just fear of dying in the war. It is something deeper and subtler, a sensation that the ground is dissolving beneath our feet. I am no longer quite so sure what I believe, or want to believe. For a moment, I am almost nauseous with the suspicion that this war is a conflict we have brought down upon ourselves, under totally false presumptions.

But then I cannot say it, not to my parents, not even to myself.

I look out across the valley, the roofs of homesteads flecking the msasa woodlands, the edges of citrus plantations. White occupation in our valley is perishing like a sheet of outworn rubber; empty houses mean gaps in our defences. My mother, now in her SPCA mode, has to deal with their abandoned cats. She is also called out to shoot rabid dogs straying in from Mozambique. We liken their increasingly frequent incursion to the guerrillas': 'That's what happens in these black states, social collapse, no vets, nothing.'

Still, many homesteaders are hanging in valiantly. Marjorie Everrite and her husband are launching confidently into a five-year coffee project further down the valley. That is what we call the Rhodesian Spirit. My mother tells me that Everrite himself, a shanky and insecure water engineer and Police Reservist, a few weeks before had got involved in a night contact with guerrillas. Another reservist, Everrite's friend and closest neighbour, had been killed in the maelstrom of gunfire. But he had not been killed by the enemy; he had somehow been shot by his own people. Rightly or wrongly, Everrite held himself responsible. In the depths of self-recrimination, he came up the hill to talk to my mother. She coaxed him up into the healing greens of the forest. They sat on what we call the Dreaming Rock, sun and shadow naved in a glade of craibia trees. He told her he wanted to kill himself.

'That's one solution,' she judiciously agreed. 'Trouble with suicide, though, is that you can't go back and change your mind.'

Everrite hasn't taken his own life. But hasn't come quite right, either.

If I could revel in this R&R, oblivious to the war, I would, but it is impossible. Daily I find myself noting the oddities of our paranoia. My father's company is demanding details of our household effects for a new compensation scheme, designed around the possibility that we'll get blown up. A huge forestry fire in distant Imbeza Estates, actually an annual controlled burn, has Mrs Schweggy exclaiming, 'Now look what the terrorists are doing to our mountain!' We read the news that the cops have netted 59 alleged *mujibhas* – guerrilla couriers, usually youngsters – who are now languishing in Umtali jail. Rotund and indomitable, Rina Smellit yelps, 'Kill them! Why are we feeding them?' I can't help feeling the neurosis is justified: guerrillas have attempted to abduct a political science lecturer, and bayonetted the Senior Janitor, on the very grounds of the University of Rhodesia. Others have attacked a house in the plush Salisbury suburb of Borrowdale. Other events are even more personal, more damaging, more infuriating. One of the daily security communiqués reveals that Laptop's father, running a commercial fishing scheme on Kariba, has been seriously wounded, and his stepmother murdered.

Of course we attempt to retain the sanity of convention in our lives. Christmas 1978 happens as usual: a few decorations glitter on the pelmets. But even here the war intrudes, a stain throwing the grain of our denials into sharper relief. One of my presents is a 'Rhopen', a ballpoint pen fashioned from two 7.62 cartridge cases, 'Genuine Doppies from the Rhodesian Anti-Terrorist War'. Straight off the range, no doubt, I sniff in my diary.

A more substantial gift is Peter Badcock's collection of pencil drawings of Rhodesian soldiery and civilians at work, *Shadows of War*. My parents have gone to great trouble to get a leatherbound, numbered-and-signed, limited edition copy: our little war is becoming a collector's item, even before it's over. I consider myself 'very, very lucky to have it'. Yet it also brings an edge of embarrassment. It is too close to being a portrait of me, or of who I think I ought to be, or who I might become if I am not strong enough. Hard-jawed veterans. Filthy heroes slaking a desperate thirst on beer. Ordinary men absorbed in mayhem. Its portraits of suffering civilians disturb; I do not want to think about those. The quotations from poets, both black and white. What is Badcock doing? Trying to make us feel guilty? Trying to put himself on the right side of some post-war political line? It seems to be so concerned about the prospects of peace, but it wants to preserve these steely war portraits, too. It is too plush, too much of an artwork. Its lush format seems already weighty with anticipatory nostalgia. I cannot indulge in nostalgia yet. I have not been released from the violent circle of the inferno. I do not know what I will face, I do not want to face some of the things this book suggests. I don't know what to do with its revelations of the 'futility of war', its dosages of pathos, its voyeuristic, almost exploitative quality. Death and destruction somehow cannot be reviled on 170 g/m^2 Saturn matt-coated art paper, in a tooled-leather, gold-lettered case.

I put it amongst my other books on the shelf at the back of my room. I realise I have been shaken to the foundations, but there is no one I can tell.

1 January 1979. I diarise my response to Ian Smith's New Year message:

From his account, the economy is holding its own but I can't see it doing so much longer. Most of his speech was devoted to attacking the Western Powers for their short-sightedness in supporting the Patriotic Front [of Mugabe and Nkomo], their weakness and deceit. He is right, of course, and no doubt his speech was geared for overseas consumption – if they have the time to listen over there – for we know all this. Yesterday or the day before a family of four were murdered near Lalapanzi, at 3 P.M. We can expect anything, any time, now. With the country sliding into the political chasm of majority rule, the terrorists are getting bolder.

Later in the day I add, with a kind of nervous jadedness:

Late evening. Exquisite light of frosted copper on the thighs of hills. The distant familiar thump of a landmine. From the reports filtering through on the Agric-Alert, an SF vehicle detonated a mine, probably on the Burma valley road. No casualties. The war is everywhere. I don't believe that the vaunted new Constitution published today, or the pusillanimous, cumbersome, compromise decision to name the country Zimbabwe-Rhodesia (which won't last long anyway) is going to change anything.

Perhaps like Badcock, trying to both bury and exploit my trials, I sum up the previous year of my life:

With the calm sunset, I can look back, evaluate. It has been a great year. In terms of the human experience it has been unparalleled. It has been unparalleled for trial, unparalleled for joy and beauty. It has been unique: Army is unique, and Mana was unique. Now it is gone, I regret all the time that has gurgled away down frivolous, dreamy gutters, frittered away while important, vital, living things lie waiting to be done, written, painted and discovered. But that is the way of life and retrospect, will always be, always. Look back, and it was a great year, and soon I will remember only the good parts. It remains only to make the next year better.

* * *

The engine of the armoured MAP growls on the upclines, my hard seat shudders, the clash of gears startles me back into wakefulness. I realign my FN's muzzle in the firing port. I am on my way back to war. I have been sent to Nyanyadzi: 'You didn't do the tracking course? Oh, well, I'll send you down to Nyanyadzi, I'm sure they can find you something to do, it's nice and *hot* down there.'

Nyanyadzi is a long way south of Umtali, the seats are bony. As usual I have compulsively relieved myself of my last remaining dollars on a couple of books. I take them out and prop them on my sun-warmed lap. John Handford's *A Portrait of an Economy under Sanctions 1965–1975* is one. It is an angry tirade against 'pseudo-intellectual' economists and 'unscrupulous' critics of Rhodesian politics. Handford seems to be arguing not only that sanctions have actually *improved* the Rhodesian economy, but also that we have effectively rewritten the science of economics.

Just as peace hath her victories no less renown'd than war, so can economic warfare have glorious triumphs, no less soul-stirring than the military variety. It is the purpose of this book to describe, step by step, how the resistance to sanctions achieved success, and doing so to enliven the story, here and there, by the Alameins, the fighter pilots, the radar systems, the convoy phasing, the commando raids, of this particular epic of war. And not one degree of exaggeration is needed to make the parallel.

'That looks a bit heavy for so early in the morning,' comments Bullock next to me. Bullock, as another failed-tracker-from-Mana, has also been banished to Nyanyadzi. 'What's the other one?'

I hold up Robert Cary and Diana Mitchell's cheaply-produced *Who's Who of African Nationalist Leaders in Rhodesia*. This is a comprehensive but dull collection of bonsai biographies. 'Jesus Christ,' Bullock jerks out, 'what the fuck are you reading *that* for?'

I shrug. 'Know your enemy. We might have to live with these people.'

'Fuck *that*. I'd sooner blow their heads off.'

'I think it's amazing that it's available at all.'

'Christ, you're an intellectual snob, you know that, why don't you read a Wilbur Smith or summing? Anyway, you'd better not read anything, we could get fuckin' ambushed out here.'

Bullock is right, of course. I glance over Willie Musarurwa's statement, in the introduction to the *Who's Who*, that 'even the most rabid' African Nationalist 'accepts the whites as part and parcel of a non-racial nation in which the skin colour of a person has no more significance than the accident that it is'.

I effect a sneer, but can't help being impressed by its apparent generosity. I put the book away, look out through the tiny firing port. A vista unrolls of dried-out fields, shaven naked as a felon's skull.

Nyanyadzi is not an auspicious point from which to launch a better year. It consists of a dispirited, largely abandoned 'Business Centre' straggling briefly along the road 100 k's due south of Umtali. A few faded buildings leak with traces of colour: Coca-Cola and Sunlight Soap adverts painted above the tottering verandas and fire-blackened windows.

By some extraordinary stroke of mismanagement, I have not been posted to an Independent Company, to which most National Servicemen are condemned. The Indep Companies are the low-life dogsbodies, cannon-fodder, free of responsibility but tedious, dangerous. I have found myself attached instead to 4 Battalion, Rhodesia Regiment, a territorial unit manned by older, largely local part-timers doing six-week stints away from their civilian jobs. They are wiser, more experienced, more relaxed, less trammelled by military bullshit. Even in the battalion's Umtali headquarters, officers slop about in green shorts and sandals. Some are already known to me. The softly-spoken storesman who handed over my heavily-oiled FN is the husband of the SPCA inspector. The paymaster is a well-known Weirmouth farmer, who this morning looked up out of a face suffused with sleeplessness and broken veins, and described himself morosely as 'a bear with a very sore head'. I paid him the 25 cents for 4RR's distinguishing hackle of blue-and-white, a pert cockade of dyed chicken-feathers to be stitched in behind the black Maltese cross of my beret-badge.

In Nyanyadzi, there is no sign whatever to support John Handford's view that sanctions have been good for the rural Africans' economy. There is no sign of an economy at all. To the east, unkempt clusters of huts amongst bleached fields and ribby livestock become progressively poorer as arable land buckles into tortuously fissured, densely-wooded hills. To the west, the flat, thorn-scrub plains alongside the Sabi River are scarcely more viable. There, the already meagre subsistence culture has been deliberately destroyed. The people have been shepherded at gunpoint into so-called Protected Villages (PVs) to starve the guerrillas of sustenance. In the immediate vicinity of Nyanyadzi, though, the human sea in which the nationalists' armed fish can swim and vanish, is all around us.

It will be our job to rectify this situation.

The Army camp itself epitomises the quality of the war. Pitched in olive-green tents on an acre of dust and paperthorns, it is spartan and flimsy. I squint at a hill looming over the camp. Too easy to park off up there and lob a few rockets into us. But I suppose there is little to be lost, other than lives, in such an attack: the camp is designed to be uprooted overnight, moved off to wherever the guerrillas have congregated next. We will move in there, clear them out, move on. Then the enemy will melt back, like a viscous toxin, into the vacuum we have left behind.

* * *

Day One. *Bullock and I have only been sent to this company because they're short of whites. The majority of the soldiers are black, but few are deemed capable or responsible enough to lead their own sticks. So one or two ES (European Soldiers) conventionally lead four or five AS (African Soldiers): the fact that these designations exist at all rubbishes the idea that the Security Forces are racially unified. Even the rat-packs are different, though most of us ES relish the 'African' staple of sadza no less than our darker companions – at least in the bush: we'd be unlikely ever to eat it at home. Given the opportunity to take 'rank without pay', Bullock wisely declines. I accept it, I prefer to be responsible for my own blundering.*

Day Two. *At 10.30 last night the news came in that Devuli Bridge, the other side of Birchenough, was being stonked. Bob Sturgeon and two of his armoured cars whined out into the darkness, coming back in an hour later without having seen anything. A scheduled Special Branch sweep is cancelled; we wait to react to something. The skin sucks at every tenu-ous breeze.*

At lunch, a callout: the heavy convoy from Umtali has been ambushed. At the camp gates, we meet the police Isuzu pick-up escort, which has sustained two hits on its Browning barrel. We move out in the Crocodile, escorted by a Ferret and two Police Land-Rovers. At the 6 km peg we debus and sweep through the bush, finding only old AK doppies and a full clip of live ammo, half-buried in sand. Oh, the ambush was at the 7 km peg? We move on, sweep again. Again nothing.

After a bit you stop thinking, 'Will it be my first contact today? Will it be my death today?' You just plod, or sit in the returning vehicle, watching the country flicking past the firing-port, the dull Africans picking at stringy crops on the vleis between the jumbled koppies, the red dust that clings to the rough welding of the armoured plating.

Day Three. *Weevilman and Co – nine of them – following the 35 who attacked Devuli, had a brief contact last night, no hits; this morning found tracks of 60-odd, and discovered that they themselves were being followed. They hightailed it out of there.*

Day Four. *Des Disparagis of the Special Branch, wiry and aggressive, his 19-year-old face etched with the assumed authority of a 40-year-old's scowl and the semblance of a moustache, leads myself, RIC Sergeant Bedd, and two constables, on the aforementioned sweep through the north-eastern villages, their bare forecourts, crumbling fields of stinkweed, ripping fences of wire and acacia branches. At the first kraal we surprise them, and pick up seven teenagers. At the second village, one. Thereafter, nobody. One old dotard, nodding off under a tree; a few sullen mourners under a traditional red flag. The school is empty, torn papers carpet the floor. There are drawings of AKs sketched on the chalkboard. 'The men are in the fields,' say the women mourners. The fields are empty as far as the eye can see.*

We come to these people with nothing to offer, no promises to make or keep. If we extend an open hand, it is only to cuff some recalcitrant youth. We possess no lever with which to extract information from them, other than fear – and unlike the guerrillas, I don't think many of us are heartless enough or dedicated enough deliberately to kill or even torture civilians for our cause. These peasants are caught between two sources of violence. We soldiers are caught between two kinds of helplessness.

Make no mistake: not one of these people will side with us. We are the insurgents here.

The news comes in that Sturgeon's mother and sister have been murdered on their Odzi farm, the father and sons all away fighting elsewhere.

Day Five. *At 2030 last night, myself, portly Rabbisch, and five AS were sent out on a four-day Observation Post (OP) partly because there's Intelligence (plausible rumours) that civilians are being re-*

cruited in the area south-east of us, partly because there are now
more soldiers than beds in camp.

By midnight we had snivelled to the base of our allocated hill, and
dossed down in a thin moon. At 0400 we struck up the treacherous
slope to establish ourselves. Sun pours down through the patchy msasa
canopies. My sweltering pores leak green camo paint. No reading-
matter, and soon no water. Do I take the whole stick down for water
(= greater firepower if we run into gooks), or just a couple (= more
clandestine)? Go to the distant river, risk the nearer borehole, raid the
kraals? Rabbisch's guts decide the issue: he is going green, vomiting. I
radio for a casevac, and we stagger him back to the main drag for
uplift.

Despite thus having compromised ourselves, we are ordered back
to the same OP.

Day Seven. *We have seen nothing. Roasted.*

There's a huge scene going on to the south: four choppers, a Lynx,
and a Dakota involved. We can hear the K-Car directing the sticks on
the ground. At least one gook killed. Comms are difficult in this clut-
tered terrain, the air filled with conflicting messages, triple-tiered relays,
constant blockages.

Day Eight. *We are recalled. Encountering some piccanins near the*
borehole, we are told that seven terrs passed this way at noon yesterday. Right under our noses. Unless these boys are lying.

Day Ten. *Escort the Umtali convoy, a huge and cumbersome serpent*
of motley vehicles: a Lynx, a Copper (Police Reserve) Cessna, two
armoured cars, three 6 Indep callsigns in attendance. Among them is
stringy Jorrock from Llewellin days, restlessly assertive behind his corporal's stripes; he orders the passengers of a two-ton truck to debus,
searches them, picks on one young man and forces him at gunpoint to
walk almost into the flames of a building mysteriously on fire by the
roadside.

Day Twelve. *Two days on a 'pillage-and-burn' sweep, clearing the*
narrow strip between the road and the Sabi, telling the inhabitants
they will have to move into PVs next week. The huts burn down all too

easily, with sickening gouts of ropey yellow smoke. Bits of furniture and suitcases stand forlornly in the sun. The PVs are a tactic adopted from the Malayan conflict of the '50s. There they worked, because they were backed by an intensive 'hearts and minds' campaign to bring the civilians on-side. Here, the thinking is generally, 'If we've got them by the balls, their hearts and minds will follow.'

Day Thirteen. *Orders have been in force that no livestock is to be permitted on the main road. Cattle found there are shot. They take the bullet between the eyes and fall like sacks of soft rock, their legs twitch and stick straight out as they roll into silence.*

Day Fifteen. *Many of us are nauseous with last night's shit-for-food. Farting miserably, we drive the 70 k's to Chipinga for a briefing on another pillage-and-burn sweep to be executed through the Lower Sabi. I have acquired a new 'stick' – five men. I suspect I will have to take a heavy hand to them. Zororo, my MAG gunner, is strong but a malingerer. Mudziwa is a surly little 'skate', likes to wear a flamboyant straw hat, and has the knotty, unkempt hairstyle of a gook. Jubasi, with his small hooked nose and petulant lip, is congenitally disrespectful. Matsororo, short, burly and piratical with his dirty green headband, is entirely vicious with the locals. 'Reliable,' Captain Beesknees called him.*

At 1530 we move out to recce the area, four sticks in two vehicles. Bullock is one of the drivers, seeming more dark-skinned and introspectively self-important than ever. He blusters that he knows the way, but somewhere off the Mount Selinda road, turning west to pick our way down the escarpment, he takes a wrong turn on a worsening road. A tyre bursts; we have no comms; so we repair the tyre and lurch on, hoping that the suspension of the cumbersome Crocs will hold, and that the road will remain passable. It does, but only just.

Day Sixteen. *We should have been out by 4 A.M., but get away at 7. Sweeping south, line abreast, burning whatever huts we find. We have four days to cover the 15 k's to Rindi. 'Int' has it that there are people living 'illegally' here – and 160 terrs. There are few huts that are not already skeletons; no people but a couple of snotty-nosed youngsters herding their painted cattle.*

Day Seventeen. *Drizzle seeped in under our bivvies all night. This morning the company commander is overhead in a light plane, lambasting stick leaders for leaving huts unburnt. The thatch is often too wet to burn effectively. Our sweep area has narrowed between hills and road, so little cross-grain is required. At one point, we hit the deck and leopard-crawl for cover as shots crack out behind us; it turns out to be rounds hidden in the thatch of a burning hut.*

Somewhere to the south, Seven-Golf are getting mortared.

Day Nineteen. *All day at Rindi Protected Village, waiting for uplift, drying out our sleeping bags before a smoky fire. The PV is the state of the nation encapsulated, a cupcake of venom and defensive suspicion. I read, from* The Terrible Rain, *an anthology of World War Two poetry I brought with me, Donald Bain's 'War Poet':*

> We in our haste can only see the small components of the scene
> We cannot tell what incidents will focus on the final screen.
> A barrage of disruptive sound, a petal on a sleeping face,
> Both must be noted, both must have their place;
> It may be that our later selves or else our unborn sons
> Will search for meaning in the dust of long-deserted guns,
> We only watch, and indicate and make our scribbled pencil notes.
> We do not wish to moralise, only to ease our dusty throats.

* * *

That is the pattern: frantic, ennervating, purely reactive, and utterly futile. We are like a brain-dead pensioner belatedly slapping at flies, succeeding only in hurting himself.

'There must be a better way to fight this war,' I write in the diary. '*Must* be.'

No one seems to know what that way might be. We blunder on, while talks simmer, and political decisions only half-understood are arrived at. Some of us even begin to suspect Ian Smith and his Rhodesian Front clique of a terrible deviousness. We have always recognised Smith as a cunning fighter – but in our vocabulary and context 'cunning' has up to now been a positive virtue. We have been pretty much in support of his manoeuvring around the stream of pushy foreign negotiators, each with his own idea of how Rhodesia ought to proceed: ineffectual Lord Pearce, lowering B.J. Vorster, deft and slippery Kissinger, somnolent Ivor Richard, naïve David Owen and Andrew Young, chisel-cold Field Marshal Carver, globular Lord Soames. Now things are changing, loyalties becoming less clear. But most us feel that Smithy is doing the best he can under intolerable pressure.

We know that we are hurtling bemusedly now towards the apotheosis – or is it nadir? – of that pressure. Elections are planned. We can be sure of only one thing: they will finally remove Ian Smith from his minority throne. We are beginning to feel like dead leaves – irrelevant, swirled in ever-diminishing circles. We are trapped in a whirlwind, caught in the centrifuge of its own purposelessness. Everyone is vulnerable and threatened, everyone fed up, tense. But no one can stop. The fighting, the pillaging, burning, destruction, go on, week after week. Few of us, if any, seriously think that these elections can be credible, since they will exclude Mugabe and Nkomo. Yet we know we can have only a political solution. Till then, we have to hold the line. We have to honour our contracts, to the living and the dead.

More than anything, these mind-numbing weeks have brought home to me my puny ordinariness. I have nothing to offer this process. There is no way I can grow inside it. But I have nowhere to run.

* * * * *

Chapter 7

Dogsbody

'WHO THE fock iss jou? You can sleep over theh, that's wheh it leaks, okay!' Leer of hilarity. My heart curls up like an old msasa pod inside me. I grit my teeth and assemble my canvas stretcher on the spot of my choice anyway.

JOC Chipinga – Joint Operations Command centre – is more substantial than the camp at Nyanyadzi was, but it's scarcely more inspirational: a cluster of low-hulled buildings suffocating inside a flimsy palisade of sandbags and wire, dominated by its radio masts, swaddled on all sides by impassable acres of smilax, bracken and knife-edged dzingai grass. Here, I join a shifting gaggle of other foot-loose soldiers the battalion doesn't know what to do with. The self-appointed tyrant of the single low-roofed barrack-room is a gargantuan Afrikaner. He sports a leer so lopsided that when he grins the left corner of his mouth ends up directly beneath his nose.

'Fockin' Four-eyes. Yuss rememmer, you's the dogsbody of all us dogsbodies, ay!'

Exactly the way I feel. And I have had enough of the bullshit, the futility, the dangerous blundering. But I think I have conceived a way beyond it. The CO is away, so I lobby our two-and-a-half-cents (2i/c, second-in-command). I know him already: an Umtali chemist whose only qualification for the job is the straightness of his spine and the assertive jut of his desk-chapped elbows. We call him Captain Apothecary. He is friendly and agreeable. I tell him I want to do a medics' course. The medical enthusiasm appeals to the man. He puts the application through.

But the course will only start in May. I will have to wait, and work.

So Walk'n'jive, a sly-looking truck-driver, five heavily-armed troopies, and myself are despatched in a Two-Five to promote the war effort. Walk'n'jive has an extravagant limp and receding straw-coloured hair, and doesn't look strong enough to handle any vehicle bigger than a bicycle. Our mission consists of negotiating 40 k's of rutted and vulnerable farm roads to a long-abandoned farmhouse – to collect a leopard-skin for the captain. The crusty relic bravely retrieved, we add to it, for good measure, a wagon wheel – probably, I speculate, a leftover from those stirring days of the Moodie treks in the 1890s.

I am intrigued by the story of Dunbar Moodie. Charlie Locker, a radio operator at Chipinga, tells me about him. Charlie says he once ferretted Dunbar's tiny pencilled diaries out of the bowels of the National Archives in Salisbury.

'Very crabbed, very cryptic. Incomplete, oh, tantalising, frustrating. But interesting, interesting.' And Charlie Locker scratches his sparse goatee. 'Poor Dunbar, always overshadowed by his bigger brother Thomas, bigger in every way. Burly Tom led the 1890s trek. You can see his gravesite, down there at the junction of the Chipinga and Melsetter roads. Hardy. Irascible. Self-serving. Dunbar, I mean. Not altogether savoury. He bristled at the Portuguese, shot lots of game, used a sjambok to hustle the locals into the TTLs. Like Ngorima. Guess what? Those are now guerrilla bases. Liberated zones! What an irony. And the tea estates. Eucalyptus plantations. All that stuff we're now spending all our energy defending? Blame Dunbar.'

The sprawling emerald tea estates still appear to be flourishing. We must be doing something right. We spend whole days driving up and down the red-earth, slippery farm roads behind a Pookie, patrolling for mines. We conduct OPs on threatened farmhouses. We lie in the rain in stupidly obvious ambush positions on the main Melsetter road – not far from the spot where, on 4 July 1964, P.J. Oberholzer was killed by the ZANU 'Crocodile Gang', perhaps the opening 'incident' of the war.

More amusing than escort duties and radio watch are the characters drifting in and out of the camp. There is the Teutonic Comic, a muscle-bound runner-up to 'Mr Rhodesia' who enjoys showing off his morning erections. There is the light-boned, evasive Pa!, a Portuguese whose explosive nickname derives from his favourite exclamation of approval, 'Tac-tics, 'pa!'

The Leer has it in for a hypochondriac, wheedling, intemperate individual dubbed Hyperjohn for his bladder's short turnaround time. Swarthy and humourless, Hyperjohn claims to have been in the RLI, the semi-élite Rhodesian Light Infantry. He is full of the rhetoric of a *Soldier of Fortune* inveterate killer.

Over our breakfast of greasy eggs and brittle bacon, he blusters: 'No, mun, if you get ambushed in a vehicle, you just stop right there, debus –'

'In the middle of the killing-field?!'

'Ja, there, out! Da-da-da, sweep, you gotta take 'em on, right there, jong!'

'Christ, Hyperjohn, you're piling out of the back of a MAP, they'll just pick you off, like poops popping out of a dog's arse! You're penga, you know that.'

'Hey!' Hyperjohn leaping up, black eyes starting out of his bearded, pouting, suddenly deep maroon face, 'Who's your *penga*? I was getting ambushed when you were knee-high to a locust, ou! I'll take you on any day, you big arsehole, hey, you wanna take me on?'

The Teutonic Comic looks down at his own massive pecs and flexes them just a little and grins almost sheepishly at the others.

'Hey, hey, siddown,' soothes The Leer. 'Hyperjohn, tell me summing.' He puts a matchbox and a match on the table. 'Using just those two objects, how wouldja get all the rabbits in Chipinga into this room?'

'Okay, okay.' Hyperjohn furrows his saturnine brow. 'Using just these two things? Okay. That's a piece of piss. You set alight all the grass in a big circle –'

'Nah, c'mon, they'll just gap it all over the place, mun –'

'Pa!? Dave?'

'Okay, how?' asks Pa!.

The Leer sticks the match into the end of the matchbox like an aerial and raises the box to his mouth: 'Calling all rabbits, calling all rabbits . . .'.

'Yussus, I gorra take a leak,' grumbles Hyperjohn.

Sometimes these idling brains do apply themselves to reality. We learn that an African man has been arrested and tried for involvement in the murder of Sturgeon's mother and sister in January.

Apparently this Af collected milk to be left at a certain farm for trans-
portation into town. Before he reached the farm on his
tractor-and-trailer he was stopped by some terrs who, it seems, told
him not to go to this farm. So he took the milk up onto the main drag
beyond, dumped it, and sat. Half an hour later the terrs ambushed
and killed the Sturgeons as they left to go to town.

The Af has been sentenced to death under martial law. Though
most of us are agreed that this is appropriate, Hyperjohn (for once)
brings up the interesting point at supper, that this was a direct result of
the Af's fear of retribution, not a studied and deliberate act of com-
plicity (though he doesn't phrase it as neatly as this), and that therefore
the death penalty is too severe. It is the way the Af thinks, he doesn't
think about sneaking off to make the terrs' presence known; he has
been threatened and will obey no matter how remote the chance of the
threat being carried out is (which is why fair elections are virtually
impossible).

The other blokes say, No, he should have warned his boss, be-
cause that's the way we think, therefore it is the way he should think,
the way a civilised person thinks.

So the death penalty is the product of the civilised way of thinking,
and until he is hanged he will never understand it!?

These speculations and desultory patrol duties aside, I am bored.
I write to my parents that I am feeling 'about as merry and lively as a
bereaved tortoise with a sore foot. Perhaps I should be thankful that
each day I sit and do nothing is another day survived, but I still don't
like it.'

I concoct a new literary scheme, a collection of directly experienced vignettes of the war.

* * *

Standing at a corner
Standing at a street corner was a soldier, eating biscuits, shabby and un-
ashamed.

He had the brim of his combat cap turned up, jockey-style, and its
edge shone black with rubbed-in dirt. Lank dark hair curled over his fore-
head and the collar of his camouflage shirt, creased, buttons missing. The

green shorts were smudged with red dust and they had a big fraying hole in the side where the pale skin of his thigh showed through. His suede boots were dusty and worn, the woollen socks crusted with burrs. His legs and arms, brown with sun, were scarred and seamed with scratches and there was still green camouflage paint embedded in them, shadows of green where it had not washed off. Only his face was clean, incongruously fresh where he had recently shaved.

He leaned his rifle against the wall, and there was russet dust in the holes of his flash hider. He hitched at his chest webbing, put down a small box of goodies. Leaning against the corner he munched steadily through a packet of Lobels' Marie biscuits, picking the crumbs off the folds of his shirt, eating slowly and automatically, without relish.

And all the time he watched the people going by with a flat, expressionless, grey-eyed fascination.

To the fat Internal Affairs man with his red-banded hat and beige uniform, who greeted him jovially, he said, 'Morning', without moving his head. The black workmen coming off shift in the building across the road he watched with suspicion, narrowed his eyes at the young one with the too-long hair and blue denims and sideways look in the yellows of his eyes. And the woman, not young, not pretty, who drove past in a blue Land-Rover and looked at him with a wistful smile, part admiring, part sympathetic, he just watched, blandly and flatly, until she had gone.

He only smiled once, hesitantly, a little embarrassed, when some small girls skipped past him, made faces at him and skittered shrieking and giggling down the pavement.

Then a dirty green truck drew up lazily, growling, on the far side of the street, towing a petrol bowser, frosted with red dust on the mudguards and the horizontal planes of the bodywork.

The soldier picked up his box and his rifle and walked quickly across to it. The driver leaned over to open the door for him and he threw his things in, climbed up and slammed the door. The truck pulled away quickly, pouring blue smoke, as though glad to get away, glad to get back to the war.

* * *

As usual, I fill the diary with reasons for general gloom. I am beginning to believe the war will never end.

26 Feb. Yesterday the price of petrol went up 20%. The political scene is not promising: intimidation and interparty dissension is evidently rife, and Chirau seems to be plugging his own line with Owen. All Security Forces are to be called up over the election period (I registered as a voter on Friday). After the Viscount disaster Security Forces have hit bases in Zambia and Mozambique and, for the first time, a big ZIPRA base in Angola. Elsewhere in the world: Britain is practically crippled by strikers, war between Uganda and Tanzania, between North and South Yemen, and a big conflict between China and Vietnam. None of which holds out much hope for mankind in general. We need to turn to a superior power. But is there one?

The issue of a superior power is only one of the many topics I discuss in the evenings with Charlie Locker. The first time I meet Charlie he is presiding over a clay model landscape he has constructed of the Chungwe Valley. The Chungwe is apparently a horrendously steep-sided, densely-wooded labyrinth of gorges somewhere north of Chipinga. It is reputedly a terr R&R venue. A massive combined HDF – High Density Force – attack is being planned. We will also be involved, it seems. We all – Captain Apothecary, the various stick leaders, the camp hangers-on – lean over the model as a good-looking major, all bustle and blue eyes, enumerates the region's more demonic features.

'We've cleared the area once before,' he rasps, 'and it looks like we're going to have to clear it again. Once more into the breach, my friends.'

'Once more into da beetch,' enthuses The Leer.

'Or we shall fill up the gap with our English dead,' intones Charlie Locker.

I don't know if I am the only one to pick up the reference or the irony, but Charlie spots my grin, and our eyes lock, and then crinkle at the corners. We are friends, just like that. It feels to me like a reprieve.

After the briefing he ambles over to talk to me, skinny shanks poking from enormous shorts. He reminds me of an angular Mark Twain, all obvious bone and lugubriously drooping eyelid. His voice is unexpectedly mellow and deep.

'You have no idea,' he says with glowing solemnity, 'how good it feels to meet someone who knows his Shakespeare.' I'm not sure I 'know my Shakespeare' at all, but I bob my head, equally grateful.

'Would you care to come over to my Establishment after supper? Desperately inadequate though it might be.' That is Charlie Locker, unfailingly gracious, modest to the point of wisdom. He has something of Tim Boot's self-containment, with none of the physical dominance.

His 'Establishment' is a wan cubicle jammed behind the Pronto's office, with just enough space for a bed (at least he has a bed). He clears papers for me to sit down. 'Sorry, I'm a newspaper editor, can't help the paper.' On a tiny locker perches a framed photo of a mellow-looking woman and two boys, and a little typewriter. It is my destiny, it seems, to be drawn to men with portable typewriters.

And a pile of books.

'What are you reading?'

'Ah, my favourite, my hero: T.E. Lawrence, *Seven Pillars of Wisdom*. Do you know it? You'll never look on a desert in the same old way again.'

'Well, I haven't looked on a desert at all so far.'

'You'll never look on war the same old way, either, and I'm sure you've seen a bit of that.' He makes me sound like a hero. 'Listen.' And he reads, a voice of measured oil, threaded with gold. Charlie Locker loves to read aloud:

Can there be profit, or truth, in all these modes and sciences and arts of ours? The leisured world for hundreds, perhaps thousands of years has been jealously working and recording the advance of each generation for the starting point of the next – and here these masses are as animal, as carnal as were their ancestors before Plato and Christ and Dostoevsky taught and thought. In this crowd it's made startlingly clear how short is the range of knowledge, and what poor conductors of it ordinary humans are.

He chuckles. 'So I guess if we're not Dostoevsky, we're the carnal masses. What do you think? Tell me about your war.'

And we talk for three hours, until it's time for his radio watch. There will more talks like this, I know. In that flimsy and soulless environment, Charlie Locker feels to me like a warmly glowing window on a drizzly night. There will be many of those, too.

In the meantime, while we wait for operations in the Chungwe to materialise, another brief tragedy ensues.

Pa! and I are about to go out on yet another all-night ambush when we are recalled. There has been a punch-up somewhere – one AS killed, two ES injured. There is uncertainty over whether guerrillas were involved or not, and our hearts grow leaden. I remember poor Everrite. The stick has holed up at the bottom of a steep valley running into Ngorima Tribal Trust Land. Ngorima TTL is by this stage a fully 'liberated zone'. Radio contact clarifies it all. They didn't run into guerrillas; they accidentally separated into threes in a gum plantation, and ripped into one another. The dead man is one of my old stick members from the Nyanyadzi camp. We have to walk some distance from the vehicles to reach him.

* * *

White phos
'Shee-it, white phos,' said Morgan.

*

You could smell it everywhere, drenched over the gumsap tang like some impossible blossom scent, a sweet, sweet reek so sharp, so sweet it seemed to reach right into the back of your neck somewhere, you could breathe the smell, like a gas, there is a corner of your senses where it clings forever. Bellman held the edge of his palm under his nose; faces lengthened woodenly, pinching to block nostrils and brain. Three feet from the body there was a blackened patch in the gum trash where the white phosphorus grenade had landed.

'Shee-it,' said Morgan, 'that was a good lob.'

'In the dark,' said Bellman. 'Mac just heard him groaning after the first burst, threw a frag as well.' Another torn patch, red earth.

'You throw a good grenade, Mac,' said Morgan.

McGeoch didn't say anything.

'It was close,' said Eric, his eyes not smiling like his face was, there was a plaster on the side of his head where they'd dug a chunk of white phos out with a knife, before it burned through to his brain.

'Us, too,' said Neil, 'it all came back over us, burnt my hand on the gun barrel trying to get out of it.' He waved a bandaged hand. 'Christ, you

bastards are lucky, I put three hundred rounds in there. Check.' Bullet-slashes in the trees, clipped branches. 'One foot lower and we'd have killed you all, hey Mac?'

McGeoch didn't say anything. He was looking at the body. Everybody turned to look at the body. It lay there with its head and torso raised improbably off the ground, as if it – he – were just easing into a sit-up. He had his hands laid across his pelvis. There was red earth on the grey-black face where he had rolled, flies at the wounds' edges. There were blackened patches on his camo and his head where the phos had found him, but it was the bullets that had killed him, stated Bellman, there were holes low on his side and big red holes under and through his arm where the rounds had gone.

'Shee-it,' said Morgan.

'Poor bugger,' said Bellman.

'He was a good guy, too,' said Eric. 'Old Enoch.'

'Well,' said Bellman, 'I suppose we'd better move.' He laid his rifle down. 'Hey, Mac?'

McGeoch didn't say anything. He was pale, grey stubble. No one moved. You could hear the soft wind in the grass.

'Well, how did it happen, anyway,' demanded Morgan. Bellman looked at McGeoch. McGeoch was still looking at the body. His jaw muscles were working under the skin.

Bellman said, 'Old Enoch here got held up at the fence moving in. We couldn't see a bloody thing. Enoch thought we'd gone thataway, so we split up. We heard the rustling, thought they were gooks, duzi here, close. So Mac tuned, hote like, 'Hey, Comrade,' and Enoch here, silly bastard, said, 'Ya!' So we ripped them. It was only when we saw red tracers coming back that we realised they were our own guys.'

'Wonder why he said Yes,' said Morgan.

'He won't fuckin' tell us now,' said McGeoch suddenly. 'Let's move.'

So we moved. We put our rifles down and wrapped the body in a brown bivvy and laid the body across the rifles, three of them, and six of us lifted and carried him like that. It was difficult and awkward, the rigor mortis wore off after a while and that broken torn arm kept flopping down out of the sliding bivvy, patches of white phos were still burning through the plastic, and Morgan said, 'Shee-it, I thought dead guys didn't bleed,' and there was thin blood sliding down his arm. It was a long, long way to the vehicle, and the death made it longer, and crossing the stream we dropped him, and you could hear the joints crunch against their death's stiffness.

'Don't worry, he's not feeling anything,' grunted Bellman, so we dragged him out again, and on.

*

'Shee-it, white phos,' said Morgan. He tried to rub a blob of jam into the woodwork of the mess table with the edge of his knife.

'Horrible stuff,' agreed Eric.

'So it was Mac who culled him, hey?'

'Yuh.'

'He was the stick leader, hey?'

'Uh-huh.'

'He must feel quite shit.'

'He hasn't been the same,' said Eric.

McGeoch came in with his food. He sat down without speaking, bowed his head and said Grace silently and quickly, and for some reason that shut us all up.

Eric said, 'How's it going, Mac?'

McGeoch just raised his fork, filled his mouth again. No one said anything until he had finished. He threw his fork down on the plate, and when he looked up and you could look into his black eyes, it seemed as though you could see all the way into the back of his head.

Eric said, 'Don't worry about it, Mac.'

Morgan added, 'It's just one of those things, Mac.'

McGeoch stood up. He took a deep breath and walked to the door, paused.

'I can still smell that white phos,' he said woodenly. He turned around, looked at us without seeing us, turned back.

'Fuck it,' he said, and slammed his fist into the wall.

* * *

I spend the better part of an afternoon helping Bubbles, the jovial and rotund camp medic, lay out dead Enoch on the mortuary slab of Chipinga hospital. I pull off the boots, extract pathetic effects from the reeking pockets. I am unable to avert my eyes from the glossy, redundant genitals lying along the bloodsmeared thigh.

At eight-thirty that evening we are off again. The Leer, Walk'n'jive, three AS, myself, and a recent arrival (named Doris for his unbroken voice and what The Leer caustically calls his 'childbearing hips') board a MAP. We are to make a midnight raid on an abandoned mission school at Ndamatara, almost 150 k's to the north, near Cashel. One of our AS has actually taught here once, and leads us amongst the eerily silent buildings, tense with moonlight. Nothing.

Nearly seven years later I will return to this very school, a teacher myself, eager to learn about the Shona communities I have been cut off from all my life. I will be the only white Zimbabwean for about 50 k's. My two years in that dusty bowl of a school, poised on the boundary between wilderness and densely populated 'communal land', will prove to be a warm and salutary correction to the arrogant racism I experience during these Army years. At a school Open Day, I will find myself sitting and eating with the father of one of the schoolgirls. He is about my age; he was once a ZANLA fighter. I ask him about that. He says simply, 'Well, it's all over now. We don't talk about it any more.' And he cocks his head rather slyly on one side and adds, 'And we're very glad to have you at our school.'

Our fruitless search of abandoned Ndamatara completed, we bum a brew at a nearby Police Support Unit base, and snatch a few hours' sleep before joining the early morning convoy back to Chipinga. By nightfall we have been briefed on Operation Chungwe. The forces gather: a rank of dusty menacing trucks, choppers on the edge of the airfield. The Police Reservists involved – all the Boer farmers from the area – are pissing it up in the canteen: 'celebrating before the ordeal', as Charlie Locker puts it.

At midnight the convoy rolls out into the cold moonlight. Our exalted task – Bubbles, Doris, myself, The Leer – is to guard six drums of AvTur helicopter fuel at a forward airstrip on the heights above our target valley. Doris, two months out of basic training, talks as if he is running the whole scene. He is one of those sad, persecuted, infuriating people who make up for some deprivation of affection in childhood by inventing elaborate, serious, but obviously untrue stories about seeing space ships and discovering dinosaur eggs. We clench our jaws and ignore his interminable chatter as we nestle Bubbles's Two-Five ambulance into a wattle grove on the edge of the windy airstrip. The strip is now little more than a subtle crease in the grass and a bald, forlorn pole, its windsock long rotted away.

By dawn the mortar teams and the OPs are in position on the bluffs overlooking the narrow gorge. Stop-groups are moving in across the valley mouth like the drawstring of a lethal bag. At seven, two Alouette helicopters thrash their way in through the clinging dawn mist to refuel and deploy the good-looking major-in-command to his forward HQ position. Two keenly glinting Vampire jets, and a more sombre and angry-sounding Lynx, go in for the initial softening-up. We can hear the grunt of bombs and judder of 20mm cannon floating up from below the hill-line. Then silence.

And that is that.

Our job done, and deprived of comms by some quirk of that buckled terrain, we uplift ourselves to a Protected Village some eight k's further on, where we are confronted by the familiar ugly mix of disaffection and relative comfort.

* * *

The Keep
This must be the most deadly job of all, the guarding of a Protected Village, one of only two white men on an all-black establishment.

And not a happy one, either, for the PV disaffects not only the terror-ists it is designed to combat, but also the people who are compelled to live in it. It shows: sullen, dark resentment as one walks by.

'Two thousand, seven hundred,' the Guard Force man tells me, a portly, talkative type, a Territorial, married, a society man, a rugby player, dragged for six weeks out of a comfortable suburban home, away from a loving brunette and paunchy living, house parties and the green fields of the local sports club, shunted off into this isolated dust-patch community with a grumpy, balding Englishman who came to Rhodesia for a holiday but never made it back to Yorkshire.

'It's a fairly average PV,' he says gaily, waving his arm across the shabby sea of brown huts, the odd brick store with peeling paint and stale bread and warm Cokes. Beyond the silver webs of the security fence the country stretches away into blueness, undulating grass and tattered stands of gaunt pine and wattle, and the cold wind blusters and whines over the highlands' naked slopes.

He turns back, looks down from the strongpoint's earth wall with its buried bunkers, to the prefab A-frame barrack rooms splashed haphaz-

ardly with yellow anaemic useless camouflage paint. 'Still,' he says, 'the Keep itself's bigger than most, a couple of extra buildings.'

But skeletal still. A muddy turnaround for vehicles they don't have (they were taken away because the last men here were in the expensive and irresponsible habit of taking a daily jaunt to the nearest town 40 k's away), a ragged volleyball net over a scrubby, worn lawn, wilting cannas along the wall, unkempt paths of blue stone between the scarred buildings.

The Guard Force man says, 'Come in, I'll make us a cup of coffee.' He is desperately jovial with having a visitor, any visitor, however brief, to chatter of sport and life elsewhere.

We go in, a cold bare room, two beds, a bookshelf, a table and bench, a scrap of sacking for carpet. An ill-designed fireplace with black smoke-marks up the front and brown up the sloping ceiling. The ceiling has a hole in it, roughly patched, and rats scratch behind the boards. In one corner, written in blue marker, the details of a past attack:

22/4/77
Duration 5 mins
75mm recoilless
3 RPG-7 rockets
82mm mortar
AK & RPD
Shithouse destroyed

The Yorkshire partner rouses himself from one of the beds, rubs bleary eyes, automatically turns on a reedy radio, grins sourly. 'Nothing to do but sleep,' he says. He is not an intelligent man, does not read much of the tattered inherited books or the week-old paper or the month-old copy of Time.

'What do you do?'

He shrugs. 'Draw up the guard list at the beginning of the week, do a clearance patrol if we feel energetic.' He grins again, wryly. 'Sleep.' No wonder they call them the 'Gonk Force'.

The last one here was studying for his B.Com, apparently. He'd been better off, had a brain and something to occupy it, except that he found the dreariness eating into his bones and his mind, robbing him of will and energy, so that he never finished anything.

'At least it's not dangerous.'

'I don't know. I suppose not, compared to the boys in the bush proper. But if we got attacked – heavily attacked – we'd get taken out for sure. None of us here are fantastic shots. Had a shoot – when was it, Friday? – only one bloke hit the bull at forty yards. My rifle doesn't even work properly. We haven't got any vehicles to escape with. And we're too isolated for anyone to come rescue us. It'd take them a week. So we just get taken out.' He spreads his hands. 'Why should I care,' he says with melancholy sarcasm, 'I never wanted to live anyway.'

* * *

Towards evening the first weary sticks are being choppered back in from the Chungwe. The HDF has turned into the GCL: the Great Chungwe Lemon. Not a single guerrilla in evidence, not a snifter of a base camp, just a few dozen shell-shocked and uncooperative civvies.

The following morning, the hapless and redfaced Major Goodlooker is ceremoniously presented with a sapling lemon tree, to be planted directly outside his office as a living reminder of his sourtasting, dramatic and costly mistake.

'Don't you worry,' growls Goodlooker. 'We haven't finished with the Chungwe, believe you me.'

That night, I ask Charlie Locker, 'Why is it that these guys make so many cock-ups? They're our commanders, they're supposed to be cleverer than us.'

'And we whites are cleverer than the gooks, right?' Charlie smiles wistfully. 'And of course we have the best educational system in Africa. And we've got the most effective counter-insurgency force in the *world*.'

'And we still can't get it right.'

'I know. Many's the patrol I've been on where we've had to rewrite our orders. No sanity. No pragmatism. But is it really surprising? We're part-timers. Chemists. Editors. Musicians. We have to make this transition, become aggressive, tactical. We're catapulted into complex counter-insurgency strategies. Life-and-death decisionmaking. How can we cope with that?'

'And I bet half of them have been promoted just because they've got the gift of the gab, or they're more bolshy than the next guy.' And

I make Charlie Locker laugh with an imitation of Captain Apothecary's elbow-jutting strut.

Our leaders are, we persuade ourselves, neither more experienced nor more intelligent than we are. They merely have more damaging scope to play out their Oedipal neuroses.

Characteristically, Charlie Locker has a book to enlighten us. It is called *The Psychology of Military Incompetence.*

> There is . . . a form of attack or mastery which must certainly be accounted neurotic. This is the compulsion to control everyone and everything which is characteristic of those who are liable to develop obsessional neurosis . . . In this way they hope to avoid anxiety by eliminating the unpredictable element in human relationships. If they can attain self-control to the extent of never being overcome by an unexpected emotion and can control others so that they cease to be free agents capable of spontaneous and therefore unexpected actions, then, according to the logic of obsessional defence, the unexpected will never happen and the unknown will never be encountered – and anxiety will never arise.

The commanding officer of F Company is just such an obsessional character. Captain John Wayne is a rangy, hunch-shouldered electronics entrepreneur, the scion of a prominent Minister under Winston Field's government. He wears impenetrable shades and a 9mm pistol slung low and back-to-front on his left hip. I like him at first because when you stiffen up to salute him he looks you up and down appraisingly for a moment and then says, 'Hi!' But the affable baring of stunted yellow teeth and air of flexible receptiveness are veneers. He turns out to be rigid, vain, domineering, impulsive, daft.

'Righto, men, listen up! Our jurisdiction is over this area, from A to P. We're going to sweep this place clean as a baby's arse, my boys! This Battalion hasn't been killing enough CTs, and we're gonna fix that up. As you know, the general kill ratio has been about 10 to 1. I don't regard that as being good enough. Together we're going to become the best killers in 4RR, you hear? They're out there; we've just gotta go and gettem. And we *will* gettem. We deploy in force, we take no chances –'

'Take no prisoners!' some stalwart enthuses.

'– Whatever. We've got the experience, we've got the brains, and if I may say so, we've got the commander. We're gonna put those fuckers over a barrel and tan their arses before the election.'

'How the devil do you tan a black man's arse, sir?'

'Ask Seagull, he's the leather fundi!' someone else says.

John Wayne remains unsmiling and staunch. 'We're gonna kill every single one we find this side of the border. There'll be no more claptrap about "liberated zones", you hear?'

No one replies.

I am being transferred to F Company. This man will be my leader. I have been given a lance-corporal's stripe temporarily, so that I can lead a stick of men into the Chungwe. I have a horrible premonition that the Chungwe will be my nemesis, have a brief vision of myself lying out in one of those burnt-out fields, bloodied, still.

That night, Charlie Locker and I talk once more. He is closer to anger and despair than I have ever seen him.

'They just don't get it. They don't see the obvious. Kill as many as possible. That is not the point, it is not the point at all.'

'So what's the point?'

He almost glares at me, but his furrowed face is softened by sadness. 'We're on the wrong track. Completely. How do we measure our success? A, the kill-rate. "Today Security Forces killed twenty-seven CTs. Seven unidentified collaborators were killed in crossfire. One Security Force member died in action." Excellent. One to thirty-four. Good ratio. We're *winning*. B, we've cleared the enemy out of this area, or that TTL. We have territorial possession. Moved everyone off into PVs. Empty country. Yay, we're *winning*. Crap. Listen to this.' Charlie reads again from *The Psychology of Military Incompetence*:

Many officers commanding counter-insurgency units deliberately try to present the situation to their subordinates in terms of conventional war. They make rousing speeches about knocking the enemy for six, and they indulge in frequent redeployments and other activities designed to create the illusion of battle. But quite apart from the tactical disadvantages which accrue, e.g. lack of continuity, they actually manage to aggravate the strains on their subordinates because they are in effect encouraging the development of characteristics which are unsuited to this particular type of operation, whilst retarding the growth of those which might be useful. In other words, they are leading their men away from the real battle field on to a fictitious one of their own imagining.

'We're not fighting a conventional war,' says Charlie. And he says it again. 'We are not fighting a conventional war. We are fighting people who live in this country. *Our* country. People we used to live alongside. People we will have to live alongside one day. What happens when we kill a "gook", or a "mujibha", or an innocent civilian in "crossfire"? All these euphemisms. We don't just kill one person. An enemy. We plunge whole families into grief. Rage. Alienation. Huge families. Extended families. We are driving our neighbours away. Our future colleagues. Leaders. Our labour force. It's stupid. The kill rate is *not* in our favour. The more CTs we kill, *the worse off we are.*'

'You're scaring me,' I tell him. 'You could get cashiered for saying this stuff. You'd better keep quiet.'

Charlie Locker is not interested in keeping quiet. 'And what justification do you have, you young pseudo-temporary-corporal, for going out and killing those people?'

'I have no intention of killing anyone,' I say, but it falls lamely, weakly. At bottom, my only job is to kill. It is all I've been trained for.

'And if you're confronted with the necessity? The whole company's going into the Chungwe. It can happen. It will happen. What if? What then?' He will not take his eyes off me, melancholy, insistent.

'Those gooks have killed as well. They could kill my folks, your kids. We've got to keep the lid on them. They're murderers, in anyone's books. Don't you want to protect your kids?'

He slumps into a wan smile. 'Of course. I guess you're right. We have to hold the line. I guess that's why I'm here. Funny how, when you try to take in the big moral picture it gets all confused. I'm confused. The Buddha said, "There is only the moment." And right this moment, I'm glad you're here. And I hope you never have to kill anyone.'

So, in the service of Major Goodlooker's unresolved Oedipal impulses, back into that cockpit of thorny torture we go.

Stickleaders Brisket, Tsoro and I are given the privilege of an airborne reconnaissance of the valleys of the Chungwe into which we will be walking. Impassable buttresses of russet sandstone plunge out of the tiers of mountain blue folding and folding away to the north, terrifying defiles of knotted bush and waterfalls. Densely wooded river lines draw the green darkness out of the gorges like the veins of embedded hands. 'Impossibly, incredibly beautiful,' I write weakly in the diary, at once daunted and enthused by that primaeval verticality, and by the equally improbable levity with which our little Cessna 180 dances on the hot and pockety currents of the sky.

At four that same afternoon, two MAPs deploy us along the increasingly familiar, mist-shrouded uplands road. We trudge past the sweet tang of the apple orchards, the wrenching sawdust and creosote smells of the sawmill and its murdered trees, and strike off the road onto a hill. We wait in silence for dusk.

For once – with one exception – I am pleased with 'my' men. Savuti is constructed of restless whipcord and quiet confidence, tirelessly alert. He has the eyesight of a vulture, is always ready with perceptive suggestions and corrections softened with humour. He is without doubt the most competent soldier I have ever encountered. I know immediately that he should be leading *me*. Our MAG gunner, Mbiti, is pale and inarticulate and enormously strong, with startled eyes and spindly legs and a powerbuilder's shoulders that twitch with unpredictable violence. My one European soldier, a blond and frizzy Rusape fitter, I judge to be as thick as a block of mukwa, but he is unpretentious and agreeable, with an openness clean as fresh linen in his face and an almost puppy-like willingness to follow.

The exception is Ncube, a slender, shifty-eyed youth who has just returned from 56 days in the Box for stabbing someone. His truculent shirking has already been the subject of a typical canteen conversation. Unable to participate in its ugliness, but unable to protest, I squirrel the conversation away as another 'vignette'.

* * *

In the canteen

Pete is on form tonight. In the flapping gloom of the canteen tent the dull light sits still across his narrow features, the teeth slant back into his mouth like a rat's, the eyes feline slits, narrow bright chinks. His voice is lazy and harsh, sibilant in the slender throat, seems to well up smooth and fluent like oil from the hollow beneath his Adam's apple.

He swallows, the shadows of the apple bob, he waves a spent match, bright sliver against the darkness.

'He should be shot,' he says calmly. 'Someone like that doesn't deserve to be in this Army. He doesn't deserve to live.'

'Him and Ngwenya both,' says Sid the canteen manager, bulbous in the corner, his face half-shadowed by someone standing between him and the light. They are all around, crowded, on Coke boxes, slumped across the floor, hanging against the tent poles. They murmur agreement.

Pete waves his matchstick deprecatingly in the air. 'Ah, ja, him as well, but Ncube mostly. He's a complete waste of rations. He's a useless soldier as well. What're we feeding him for? All he does is cause trouble.'

'You get them in every camp,' says Mike, tall in the door.

'Exactly,' says Pete. 'If it weren't for him and Ngwenya this graze problem would never have come up. We'd still be getting our rations and they would still be getting their AS rats. Which is the way it should be. Why should they get the same food as us? They don't need mukiwa graze, they're blacks.'

He slots the match between his rodent's teeth, glares cat-like at nothing. No one says anything. If they agree there's no need to say anything, because Pete has said it all. If they don't, there is something in Pete's bland assertiveness that keeps their voices still.

'No,' says Pete, plucking out the match. 'He should be shot.' He looks up suddenly, a new interest springs from his woodenness. 'Whose stick is he in? Dave? You must shoot him, Dave. Just accidentally. Push him over a cliff.'

Dave, gargoyle on a box, chuckles. 'If I'd been his mother, I would have done it at birth.'

'And Ngwenya,' says Pete.

'And Sibanda,' says Sid.

'And Sibanda. In fact, the whole bloody lot of them should be shot. We'd win the war faster without them.'

'We'd win the war faster without the gooks,' points out Clive, eyes bright above blond beard.

Pete says blandly, 'Well, they're also black. So they must die. All blacks must die. Civvies as well.'

He broods a while through his narrow eyes, through the silence.

'We're too soft, I tell you. We must go in there and just cull. We should send the Ferrets through the TTLs. Just pull everything that moves. Send the Air Force in, take out the townships. Bomb Sakubva, forty thousand hotes, wham! Open season.'

He prods the air with his match. 'It's the only way we'll win this war, I'm telling you. They're all in with the gooks, just cull the lot. Hitler would've. They should never have done away with Hitler. Once Hitler had finished with the Jews and the Russkies he would have turned to Africa, he hated blacks. They're an inferior race. So he would have wiped them out. Then think what a better place the world would have been.' And he lets that one sink in, in the quiet.

Then he says, 'Or we should get Amin in here. He's killed a couple of million in Uganda. That's half our hotie population already. Imagine how our problems would be lessened.'

'I dunno,' says Sid, 'I wouldn't want to have Amin ruling me.'

'Who said anything about him ruling? He'd just be the Doctor Field Marshal of his very own assassination squad. We give him a couple of Noddy medals and he'd be only too pleased to add a few more hundred thousand skulls to his collection.'

Which raises a laugh, low but enough to break the ice of Pete's monologue.

'But that's the sort of thing these blacks do,' insists Pete. 'They're ten times more savage than the civilised white man can bring himself to be. That's our problem, we're too civilised. That's why I reckon that if there's a civil war in this country we should just stand aside and let them at it. Eventually they'd wipe each other out and we could have majority rule again – white majority rule.'

And the listeners chuckle again. Sid says, 'No, he's right. What we need here is a black Company Sergeant Major. He'd sort these troublemakers out.'

'We would never have a graze dispute with a black CSM,' agrees Clive.

'Not a chance,' says Roy darkly. 'He'd have put Ncube on dry rats.'

'That's what we should do,' enthuses Clive, 'put him on dry rats for the rest of the camp.'

'Ag, just shoot the sod,' says Pete, flicks the match away and follows it out into the darkness.

* * *

When darkness falls we hit the road and walk for two-and-a-half hours until a pregnant, phosphorescent moon lifts its belly above the eastern ridge. We snivel into a gum plantation: three sticks, sixteen men in all, crunching through the knee-deep, acid trash about as quietly as a herd of Centurion tanks. We settle in a wide three-sixty to sleep. In the morning we find a thicker patch of scrub to hide in, try unsuccessfully to make radio contact with somebody – anybody. We bemoan the idiocy of Goodlooker's orders. Who in his right mind would send a stick of five men (mine) alone into the bottom of a valley where no Security Forces have been for seven months, with a near-certainty of no comms?

'The fucknut must have had a lobotomy instead of a baptism,' Mukwa growls with unusual eloquence.

'Jeez, we didn't realise you knew that word, Muks!'

'What word?'

'Lobotomy,' I say.

'Baptism,' says Tsoro.

'Fucknut,' says Brisket.

We fiddle with the locstats, work out a plan so we can at least be within support distance of each other. In the late afternoon, we sneak away along the edges of gum plantations all aslant with pollinated sun and zithering with bees. At dusk Tsoro, an intelligent, melancholy prankster of a man, branches off towards an OP position on one of the ridges. Brisket and I move further north, startled by galumphing, suspicious cattle. We skirt the Keep with its yapping dogs, music intermittent on the wind, and Oh-so-welcoming lights (concealing, we know, only those miserable draughty rooms and smoke billowing back down the chimney). At nine we hole up in a thicket of elephant-grass and ripping wait-a-bit thorn, and sleep.

The moon is high at four in the morning when we head west again, blundering over half-ploughed fields and fences, until softer miombo woodland envelops us, and we split up. Brisket grins a farewell through his spaced-out gravestone teeth. I feel bereft. Down in the gorge (it is thought) is an old CT base camp. It is my job to find it. With Tsoro in position on the south ridge, Brisket overlooking from a promontory to the north, we feel at least observed, if not exactly safe. Down we go.

Loose black forest soil drops stones out from under our feet, smilax rips our shirts, rocks grow slick as oiled ice with seepage and peeling moss. Matted bracken and sickle-thorned creepers force us hacking and cursing back up the sides, arms aching from thrashing through branches and wrenching free our snared rifles. Down into a tributary, up the other side. We find a semblance of zigzag path. It leads us to a tattered thatched shelter beside a surprisingly well-kept garden, complete with neatly-coiled green hosepipe. We are still a kilometre from the alleged base camp. The path peters out in a patch of stinkweed. We blunder out through neck-high bracken and onto the msasa-covered hillock where the camp is supposed to be, sweep through, line abreast; around; back. No base camp. We collapse. It has taken until midday to achieve this emptiness.

In the middle of our lunch Brisket radios huskily: 'One Alpha! AMA, in grey and brown, heading your way from the south, over.' We crouch for an interception, but the interloper spots us first and is gone.

'A gook!' insists Mbiti, 'A gook, that one.'

Giving up the chase, we pound up the opposite slope onto a subsidiary spur to OP and rest our aching backs. The afternoon creeps. I curse my oversight in not bringing a book.

The following morning finds us perched on the edge of a vertical drop overlooking the upper reaches of the southern arm of this valley. The Chungwe River wriggles down and away across towards the Tanganda. We can see the main Chipinga road and, beyond that, maybe twenty k's away, the snooker-table baize of the lower Sabi irrigation schemes.

At ten we spot three women skulking around a small banana grove below us, putting blankets out in the sun. Tsoro has also picked up a woman carrying a basin full of cooked mealies, evidently feeding someone outside the PV. We wait. Just before lunch Savuti's infallible eyes spot six men moving into a tree-shaded cattle kraal near a cluster of abandoned huts. Two of them appear to be mujibhas, young porters or messengers. One of the men is carrying an RPD machine-gun.

My heart pounds. Finally, finally, I am doing what I am supposed to be doing, I am not playing at soldiery now. At last it is for real.

John Wayne begins to move in everyone he can lay his hands on.

Brisket is to come down off his ridge and into the attack while we direct him in. Tsoro is pulled over into an ambush position at the head of the valley, on the main route up into the PV. Two other sticks are to provide stops at the bottom of the valley, but they seem to be taking all day to be trucked in and marry up. Goldilocks is to be dropped on the Tanganda River, but he'll have some horrendous hills to negotiate before he can be of the remotest use.

Brisket takes an hour and a half to get onto our ridge, flounders around for a while trying to get the gooks' position clear – then moves with astonishing speed. We see nothing of him. As if from beneath the earth itself, he initiates the thunderous contact. The valley is stunned with gunfire. Two CTs gap it down the hill. Mbiti rips them with the MAG. It's 800 metres but he's as accurate as a cobra strike. His tracers set off a vigorous blaze in the grass. There is no return fire. A smoky silence falls.

Brisket starts sweeping. John Wayne turns up in the PRAW plane and strafes the trees downhill with its Browning, with no visible result. He keeps ordering Fred to do this and do that, then saying, 'Okay, take over, Freddie,' then saying, 'Freddie, head east from where you are –' and I have to interrupt, 'Negative, ignore Sunray, if you head east you'll get ripped to pieces in open ground,' and so on. We wish the cowboy would shut up and go home and just let us get on with it.

We gallop down into the valley ourselves to sweep up the riverline. We flush out nothing more dangerous than a duiker, turn, and pad warily down through the fire-blackened grass to group up with Brisket at the banana grove.

One of the mujibhas lies in the kraal, his guts poured out amongst broken bottles, abandoned shoes, a miner's helmet, cowdung. He was dying very slowly when they reached him, says Brisket, and told them there were fourteen CTs in the area. Doris, furiously compensating for his childhood, was the only one with the nerve to finish him off with a bullet in the head.

I silently thank Christ it didn't fall to me.

Following up tracks in the morning we find the body of the second mujibha, his clothing charred in the grassfire. He could only have been nine or ten. I wonder who will find him. Perhaps his own father. Feeling hollow beneath the breastbone, I think about how it would be for him.

* * *

The cry

I am lost. I am poor. I am nothing.

Last month I was free. Last week I was wealthy. Yesterday I was a father. But today I am nothing.

I was free, last month, and I walked with my fine cow in the hills, and she gave me milk. I sat in the warm sun and took the milk from her, and it was good. I grew some mealies before my house, and they grew tall and strong. I cooked them slowly, and ate them, and they too were good.

The terrorists came, the gandangas.

They said, Give us food, we need food.

I said, Surely, I have much milk and maize, and I will give you some.

They did not say, Ndatenda, Thank you. They went over the hill to the house of Peter Takadera, and said, Give us food, for we are hungry.

And Peter Takadera replied, No, I have no food. I have enough for myself only.

The next day the body of Peter Takadera lay as a fallen tree before his door, and his wife cried. Surely these men are very powerful.

Last month the white soldiers came.

They said, You have been giving food to the gandangas. You must move to the new Keep.

I said, But I cannot move. How can I move? This is my home, these are my fields.

You must move, they said, and they burned down my house. They too are surely very powerful.

I must take my cow with me, I told them.

You cannot keep a cow there, the soldiers said. You must leave it here, and you may come and see it every day, and your fields also. But at night you must sleep at the Keep.

So I had to build a new house among many others, very many, and around them all a high fence, and the soldiers walk there. It is very far from my kraal and my cow, and each day I must come there, and each day return to the Keep, over the hills, and I am very old.

I am very old, and my son is very young. He came to me and said,

Father, the gandangas say we must give them money. They say the white men are bad because they take us away from our lands and our homes, and they take away our schools, and put us in villages with fences. If we will give them money, they will free us from the white man, and build us new schools and break the fences.

My son, I said, I have no money, and I do not want money. I do not want anything to do with these gandangas or the soldiers or the white men. I am very old and I no longer have the strength for these things. If they force me to do things, then I must do them. But if not, I shall stay.

They say, said my son, that if you do not give them money they will come and kill you. And his face became hard, hard like the stones of the riverbed.

I sold a little milk, and I gave the money to my small son, and he would take it to the gandangas.

They will write your name in a big book, he said, and he was proud. I did not see him often any more. I have business, he said.

Last week I became very wealthy, for my cow bore a child. Peter Takadera had a fine brown bull with horns that curved round to the sides of its head, and this bull was the father. One day, Peter once told me, those horns will grow into its head and it will die, and he was sad.

But last week I was happy. Soon I would have two fine cows to give me heavy milk and joy, and perhaps some day I would have three, and I would be truly wealthy.

Yesterday I began the long walk to my kraal. I heard many bangs in the valley, down where my kraal stands, and though I was afraid I tried to hurry to see, but I am very old and very slow.

And when I reached my kraal it was very still and the air was bad and heavy.

My cow was dead. My small, so beautiful calf, was dead, and the flies buzzed over it. There was a dead gandanga there, too. And beside him lay my son, very small, and he was dead also, and the soldiers were moving away down the valley.

Today I have nothing. Peter Takadera's big bull looks at me from the field, and he cries. Life hangs from my head heavy as horns, and one day they will grow back into my head and I will die.

* * *

We sleep on a windswept hilltop, all such wrestlings with conscience and vain imaginings swamped with real exhaustion and fragmentary dreams and the creaking terrors of pre-dawn guard.

It is Brisket who finds the base camp. In a well-camouflaged cave, large wooden trunks are packed with neatly-pressed clothing, linen, beads, and an assortment of oddities: saws, aphrodisiac pills, a rusted bicycle, a telephone, a bunch of skins, a tape-rule, a chair, two AKM magazines, oddments of CT webbing, a comprehensive Tanzanian medical textbook, balls of wool, Rhodesian-printed English language textbooks – and notebooks containing lists of the Mutema Detachment Committee members, 'How the Committee Works', receipts of contributions, names of supporters.

'Jesus, look at all these collaborators! How can they expect elections to work, with this kind of intimidation going on?'

The AS pile in and cram their packs as tight with loot as they can, or stuff both the loot and their packs into even bigger holdalls they discover. A gallon of petrol proves useful in setting fire to what we aren't able to plunder. The remnants of a goodly number of people's desperately hoarded material lives goes up in the thick, dull-reeking smoke that scatters squeaking bats from the cave's mouth.

The Company Sergeant Major wants the bike. One of the trackers carries it out in the hope of some reward.

So a caravanserai of overburdened and idiotically colourful plunderers plods back up to the beetling heights, collapsing in a slumbrous three-sixty, the peeling bike – now called the 'K-Car' – propped up incongruously in the middle. We make the final radio report for the day. My heart warms to hear Charlie Locker's baritone over the air. Tired though he is, Fred Brisket is irrepressible.

> *Fred* (callsign One Foxtrot): One, hello One, this is One Footrot.
> *Charlie* (callsign One): One Fred, One Graham, go ahead.
> *Fred*: Roger, we've reached the top of this hill, and there's a guy up here at a gate and he won't let us through, over.
> *Charlie*: Confirm a guy at a gate?
> *Fred*: That's affirmative. His name is St Peter and he won't let us through his gate.

Charlie: Ja, roger, we've heard of this guy. Confirm he's wearing webbing?

Fred: Affirmative. He's also got an AK. Can you ask Sunray what we should do?

Charlie: Roger, can't you jump on a passing cloud and bypass him?

Fred: Negative, it's a clear day, over.

Charlie: Ah, roger that. Well, you realise you were supposed to go south, not north?

Fred [consternated]: Nuh-negative, say again?

Charlie: Roger, you were supposed to go *south*. If you'd gone that way you'd have found a little red man with horns and a fork, roger?

Fred: Oh, ja, roger, that's all right then, we've already eliminated *him*.

* * * * *

Chapter 8

Under Fire

CHARLIE LOCKER is sitting on his bed, bare-chested, cross-legged, a white towel around his waist. He grins with relief as he sees me.

'You have survived.'

'Oh, yes. There was actually not much danger.'

'There is always danger. Did you tell your parents about the contact?'

'I didn't want to. Then I couldn't help myself. Even though it was disappointing.'

'You mean, no kills.'

'Just a couple of kids, boys. Sad.'

He looks at me very straight, the drooping eyelid makes the stare more intense. 'You're not sad. You cannot actually admit them to the family of Man, can you.'

I feel myself heat up, shame mingles with anger. But I cannot reply. I say instead, 'You don't have a violent bone in your body, do you.'

He softens again, smiles. 'I'm not Gandhi. Who knows what circumstances will call up violence in us? We don't even begin to know what violence we have in us.' He gets up suddenly and gives me a lingering, bony hug. I have never been hugged by a grown man before, as an equal.

'You don't know how glad I am that you're alive.'

'It isn't over yet,' I say grimly.

Goodlooker and JohnWayne have still further harebrained schemes for the Chungwe. Now they want to put us in for a ten-day OP. Then they will make of the Chungwe valleys yet another no-go zone. More hut-burning. Move the people into the PVs.

Kill if necessary.

* * *

We perch ourselves on the edge of a particularly spectacular cliff. Two hundred feet of russet, falcon-haunted rock plummet to a well-populated valley below. The cries of babies and the demented brays of donkeys feather up on the smoky air. Far in the distance we can see the unlikely silver arch of Birchenough Bridge, vivid in the beginnings of a copper-and-burnt-sienna sunset. The lowering world looks as if it is curling up at the edges.

Through the strange and livid light filtering through the broad-leaved muzhanje woodland, an African man stalks. His head is down, he is looking for herbs maybe. He walks right into us before he sees us. He looks slightly mad in the eyes, turns all but inarticulate with fear. But he speaks more energetically after Mbiti gives him a swift punch in the face. In between snorting out gouts of bright blood from a broken nose, he admits to living in the valley where we found the base camp. He laments that the soldiers have burned all the locals' clothing: '*Zonke*, everything.' I think, *Good. He is obviously a collaborator, if not a pukka CT.*

We guard him closely all night, and walk all morning to deliver him up to the PV, hindering the possibility of his escape by making him carry my overstuffed pack. He is an old man.

I feel no sympathy – or I am pretending to feel none.

For three days we skulk on a more southerly, less exposed ridge. Nothing. We nurse our diminishing motivation. John Wayne is away somewhere. Between watches I read, and write. I sketch out the first version of that little essay I call 'For the Experience', as if the war were already over. I write:

This is what you learn in the Army: joy and fear, honour and degradation, courage and humour and tolerance, discipline and fastidiousness and tactics, though these are more valuable to the soldier than to the human being, even if the soldier and the human being are one and the same, and one inevitably creeps over on the other.

Nowhere is my confused ambivalence – as it were – clearer.

I write of appreciating simple luxuries and ease, of encountering all the 'wise people and stupid people and crazy people and black people' in this 'alien and violent society', of the paradoxes of the 'sad-eyed businessman killing for his life, bloody corpses in a spectacular landscape, ribald jokes in the middle of a contact'. These are things, I conclude, which 'catapult life into a newer, truer and infinitely wiser perspective'.

But I know in my heart that it is all a little desperate, a little premature, and a little more comforting than true. I know that I am writing of desired, not actual, belief. I want to be experienced without having suffered the pain.

And I jot down, not yet knowing what to do with it, the verbless sentence: 'That poised, elemental, decisive moment when you hold life cupped in your hand, to crush it or let it fly.'

Though I have not yet experienced any such moment.

On the fifth day of the patrol John Wayne comes back on the air and orders us back to the ridge on which we'd encountered the herb-gatherer. He is very excited: the herb-gatherer's name is on the list of guerrilla supporters Brisket found in the cave. John Wayne is positive we will find another base camp there somewhere.

Right, and Leonid Brezhnev, too, I suppose. Base camp my arse, with not a drop of water for kilometres . . .

'Now you damn well make sure that entire ridge is clean as a baby's bum,' his voice crackles. 'Then you're going down into the valley.'

As the dawn sun begins to tip the leaves of the muzhanje trees with frosty gold, we start quartering the flat ridge-top. We are as tense as violin-wires. Tsoro's stick has been moved in a kilometre to the east, sitting tight while we comb.

Without warning – no sounds, no smell of smoke, no trace of premonitory path – three huts loom up through the trees and the silky light. As if in a dream, I see my hands make the signals, *Get into line abreast, Mbiti spread out, move in*, at first it all seems desperately slow, then it races away with us, a thin shout, running figures, I think a boy, two, perhaps a man, is it a man, a woman, running, Mbiti's stubby legs splay and set and the MAG hammers out and I follow, scarcely aiming, the FN snapping with the sound of a breaking bone in my hands, one of the huts swirling into flame, and I hear as if from a great distance my own voice, 'Go through, go through, Muks, that hut, grenade, go!' and the crump of the grenade and then we are on the far side of the huts, in a shocked silence, looking down at the girl.

She is dying. Her face is down against the earth, making no sound. Her back and legs gape scarlet and deep maroon with terrible wounds, the MAG's rounds, perhaps my own, surely my own. Perhaps my own. A nick in her bared buttock leaks a grotesque smile of ivory fat. Even as I bend to her, she seems to shrink into herself, and dies.

I try to roll her over, 'Maybe she's got some ID on her.' Stupid idea. Her skirts are rags, reeking of woodsmoke, they rip in my hands, her weight seems to weld her to the earth. I stop.

'Pity,' I say. 'You could have had a good time with her, eh, Ncube?'

I know instantly that speaking is a mistake. Ncube's eyes are fixed in his head, his dark skin dusted with grey. I don't think he has ever confronted such a death before. I wonder briefly what I look like to him.

Baboons are barking further along the cliffs. 'Two boys,' says Mukwa, 'I saw them, little kids.'

'Fuck, we're well and truly compromised now.'

'Anyone see any men?' None.

One hut is already almost gutted with the fire. We search the other two. There is nothing incriminating. The place was evidently the home of a witchdoctor, probably our herb-gatherer. One hut holds a large collection of bits of bone and skin, unidentifiable odds and ends wrapped in plastic, powders in bottles – and some money, including ancient King George sixpences, which Mukwa promptly pockets. In the other, a large number of string traps, tins of grain, and a programme for a Salvation Army Dedication Service dated September 1970. *Jesus, was the man a Christian?*

We set the huts alight, quickly traverse the rest of the ridge. Nothing.

That evening, my eyes straining in the last of the light, I write in the diary. I have to write it.

This morning at about 0700, as we move along the ridge, we stumble on two huts among the trees. I see two, a man and a youngster, gapping it, Mbiti and I shout, 'Mira! Wait!' a couple of times before opening up. We sweep through, find we have killed a girl, perhaps sixteen or seventeen, hit three or four times in the back. No comms with anyone for twenty minutes. What if it had been a serious contact, for Chrissake? Where the other two went is anybody's guess.

Looking down at the still, smooth, blood-torn body of the girl, should I feel joy? Should I feel remorse? In fact I feel very little of anything at all.

Strange, looking back, how detached the moment of action seems, how almost of its own will the rifle leaped to the ready, how the bullets sprang it seemed of their own accord, how I never even noticed the recoil.

Even as I put it down, I know I am not being honest. What is this self-consciousness of the present tense? Why do I translate, '*Mira!*' (we certainly did not actually shout in English)? Who am I writing for? Is that truly a quiver of religious apprehension, that we might have attacked the establishment of an upright Christian man? So angry over the loss of comms, my bemused desire to distance myself from my actions? A man, why do I write there was a man, did I see a man?

But I do not change the diary entry, then or later. At some subliminal level I know that the gaps in memory, the excuses, the lies, are necessary. I cannot deal with this without them.

Much later, I will write to my parents:

So back north we went, and there walked into two huts which shouldn't have been there, a man, woman, and youngster fled, disobeying orders to ~~flee~~ stop, so we opened up on them and the woman (whom I actually hadn't seen) was killed. She turned out to be (to have been?) quite young, seventeen or eighteen. I suppose one should feel remorse at this sort of thing, but I really feel nothing at all, no joy, no sadness, deadness only.

Who am I protecting, with this sanitisation? My parents, myself, all of us. I have said that guilt is a room we have been shut out of. But we continue to build the walls above us, a redoubt of willed and willing numbness and silence. I am imprisoned in my freedom to kill. My doubt curls up in yellow dismissal, like thatch under fire.

That night in the thickets of an anonymous Chungwe gully, I sleep dreamlessly.

JohnWayne orders us down into the valley. I look over the edge and almost ask him for a couple of hang-gliders. The sky is clear and innocent. It is 6 April – my mother's birthday. We try to find a path marked on the map down one of the defiles, but lose it, have little choice but to keep going, down through the tangles of undergrowth, between the towering buttresses of our terror.

With Tsoro directing from the bluffs above, we begin burning huts. Almost all the inhabitants flee as soon as the first gouts of thick yellow smoke go up. At one complex a surprisingly spry old man is busy removing valuables from his huts. He knows all too well what is coming. He earnestly advises us, 'This is a good road, take this road.' Suspicious. We take a different path. But our necessary route is all too obvious. Plumes of roaring flame advertise our progress as clearly as neon on a Las Vegas casino. We are tense with expectations of ambush.

We are climbing a narrow path towards another cluster of huts and surprise a young woman there. She seems less surprised than we are. She stands strangely still. Perhaps she simply has had no time to flee. Perhaps she has remained for a purpose. She begins to lament shrilly that all her family's grain for the season is in a raised wooden granary next to these huts. I apologise, tell her she will have to move to a PV, we will have to burn the thatched granary but she can come back and get the grain, she can shovel it out of the granary for now. This will take time, my men look restive. I wave them into a three-sixty.

As she begins to spade frantically with a wooden pole, rustles in the bush to one side snap us round. Cattle are moving there, and Mbiti says quietly, 'Don't shoot, it is cows only.'

There are more than cows. There are two men, dressed in the classic dark denims of the CT, bowing away into the shadowy bush, melting away. I am looking through the legs of cattle, I do not want to shoot the cows. I do not want to shoot. I see the men. I know that I have seen them. But I do nothing, say nothing. I am spooked. No one else appears to have seen them; I am prepared even to doubt my own eyes; I can take the sighting with me to the grave.

I put nothing of this into the diary. I will not, cannot, admit to another, possibly fatal, error of judgement.

But I also know that I will never forget it.

The consequence of my silence isn't long in coming.

* * *

The contact

He has always dreamed of it. Five of them, they walk out into the gold sunlight of the clearing, alert, but the bushes are too dark for them to see him. He lets them reach the middle. There is no cover, they haven't a chance, calmly and with infinite satisfaction he cuts them down, one by one as they run and roll.

But when it comes it is not like that. The only thing that is the same is the bright sunlight.

At first he can't tell where the firing is coming from, even, in the initial seconds, that he is being fired on at all. He is speaking on the radio, the snapping of bullets doesn't register, for a moment his mind runs wild, then suddenly his stick has passed him on the hillside path, skidding into cover they are already firing, and he flops face down behind a tree, diving downhill his pack comes over and hits him behind the head. He pulls off a few rounds vaguely, he can't see for branches hanging down in front of him, for the sun setting over the opposite ridge. He can hear the light crack of the AKs across the river, bullets snipping through the trees above him.

He thinks, You die now.

He gropes for the telehand of his radio, he's dropped it and has to pull it out from under him by its lead. He yells into it, but no one answers. They are still firing, and the MAG is hammering to his left, and it occurs to him that his sensitive ears are going to be singing for a week. He calls into the telehand again. Nothing. There is a fresh spatter of bullets among the leaves, dust springs and drifts. Too high again.

He says to himself, You will not die today.

A calm settles over him. He levers himself into a sitting position, pulls his cap down over his eyes, clips the telehand back onto its strap. He sees puffs of smoke. He fires, a branch floats down in front of him. The firing carries on. He thinks, This is no damn good.

'Rob, put a rifle grenade in there.' Rob works quickly, efficiently. There is renewed firing from the other side, this time he sees the flashes, about ten of them. Rob's rifle cracks, the grenade roars, a gout of earth, too far.

Then Mbiti calls, 'You see them?'

He sees them, running left.

'Flanking attack!' Mbiti's eyes are wide, whites all around, the mouth slack. Mbiti is afraid, and the fear comes flooding back over himself.

He says, 'Let's get back up on that hill.'

They hump abandoned packs, push fast up the hill slope. His legs are

148

cramping, must eat more salt, he tells himself. He waits for the bullets to come, slam into the back of his pack. The fear grows greater with the retreat.

The radio crackles. He pants, 'Wait out,' just let me get onto high ground, for Christ's sake. They get there, watchful, three-sixty, wait for it. The drone of an aircraft. Listen, you coward, gooks don't make flanking attacks. Get onto the edge, look for them. That guy up there is going to know you ran for it.

'Binoculars.'

He sweeps the hill. Nothing. You're all right. Calm and responsibility come sweeping back. Anyone hurt? How many rounds? A quick sitrep, Copper Six-Two, this is Seven Delta, roger, figures one zero Charlie Tangos gapped it west along the river, north bank. Roger, I have a map out, do you have me visual?

The darkness falls quickly, blue and bruised purple. We'll base up for the night, get onto tracks in the morning.

He sits down on his pack, and though he has never smoked a cigarette in his life he feels the urge now, he picks up a stick and 'smokes' it. He grins at Rob. Rob grins back, gives a thumbs-up.

'You did OK,' Rob whispers.

He shrugs.

You coward, he says, but silently.

* * *

With no injuries sustained except Mbiti scorching his wrist on the MAG barrel, we are extracted by truck the following morning. We rest. I am conscious that I have led my men nearly into catastrophe. I can scarcely speak. I watch the CSM, who is riding around the base camp on the refurbished 'K-Car' bicycle. It is now 'mineproofed' with water in the tyres and a miniature sandbag under the saddle, a military numberplate up front, a sign on the rear mudguard advertising 'Seagull Rolls Royce', its own radio and callsign, a sputnik aerial clattering at the end of a mineprodder like the appendage of some futuristic unicorn. It is very funny. But I cannot laugh.

Charlie Locker misinterprets my grim silence.

'You can't live on heroism. Heroism isn't a food. It's a drain. It's a succubus. A deception. Don't tough it out.' He quotes Oscar Wilde at me: ' "It's not so much what you do that is evil, but what you become because of it." ' He begs: 'Don't go hard on me. On yourself. Don't shut down. You're a poet.'

'That's not it,' I say. But I cannot tell him what it is. I am not still entirely sure myself what it is. I am conscious that I have created a stiffness between us. I do not allow myself to be hugged. In the diary I write with miserable, muddled hyperbole:

> *Now I feel almost as bad about shunning Charlie as I do about the girl. He is such a beautiful man, he only wants to help. But he's never been through anything like this. He doesn't understand anything. Was she beautiful, too, in her way? I didn't notice, how could I? I am his Judas, I'm his crown of thorns.*

I cannot, in short, admit to Charlie Locker – or even to myself – that I have shamed him; that his very warmth, his moral intelligence, cut me like a blade; that I can't see where to fit the beautiful into my world now. Laughter is a falsehood; even friendship is an avoidance of the dank truth of myself.

Then Charlie Locker is gone, finished his stint, gone home to Bulawayo to run his newspaper and his family. I come back from some inconsequential escort duty; the Establishment reeks with another Pronto's presence, corpulent, guttural, leaking beer. No chance for the decent farewell. Again. Though I know, somehow, that Charlie Locker hasn't left my life, the evening still feels heavy on the nape of my neck as I walk across camp towards the troopies' canteen.

And of course my old mate Bullock chooses this moment to materialise out of nowhere and tell me that Tim Boot is dead. He was taking part in another elephant cull in Wankie. Someone fluffed his shots, a wounded bull found Tim in his sights, gored him, lifted him high, dashed him just once to the bloodied ground.

'Bad,' says Bullock, pressing his lips together. 'That's very bad,' which is what one says in such circumstances.

I walk away from him, down the dirt road alongside the silent airfield, where there's only the dzingai grass and heavy dust and nothing to impede the hard cold wind or tears.

No narrative, I tell myself. Only the moment. No narrative. Only the moment, this frightened grasshopper, this late sky stretched in its stupid grin.

Later, as I snivel down onto my fraying stretcher to sleep – something hard beneath my pillow. A book. *Seven Pillars of Wisdom.*

* * *

Perhaps we should not be surprised to find people still trying to live on the floor of the Chungwe Valley when we return. But we are.

I am determined to cuff this patrol. My medics course approaches, I don't need any more excitement. There is little left to burn in the valley anyway.

In a grey mood, I do the minimum to make it look as if I'm finishing the job.

A little old man with tractor-tyre sandals and long matted hair squats before his tattered hut, obsequious, whining, He has no home, no place to stay, no family, no relations, he is just 'following the forest', he rubs his thumb aimlessly along the blade of his bulbous-headed axe. Helplessly we wave him away. Another white-bearded man pleads that there is no food in the Keep, he has to wait for his crops to ripen. Again, we can only tell him what our orders are. I am beginning to feel haunted by these old men, rising like a series of ghosts to remind us of our consciences, of vulnerability, of the greater sadness of all our wars.

Meanwhile, we are getting contradictory radio information about whether or not this valley is actually supposed to be included in the no-go area. John Wayne tells us to burn on.

We corner a woman and a pair of youngsters on the edge of a field. She will not speak. Without warning Mbiti clubs her down with the butt of his MAG. The blow to her head makes almost no sound at all. She sits down abruptly. She tells us then there are seven CTs in the area. How can we know that this is true? Maybe she just thinks this what we're after, she will say whatever will shake us off. Mbiti has confidence in his violence. 'She is telling the truth, surely.'

In any case, the tension cranks up another notch. We swivel the muzzles of our rifles constantly between the trees. An hour later Savuti spots five men on the far side of the river, maybe a kilometre away. One is sitting in a tree. 'They are young men, gooks, sure-sure.'

I believe him. I want to believe him. There will be no mistakes this time. The heart begins to race, but thoughts come clear and cool. We quickly map out a route through dead ground, begin to run, and plunge down the slope, cursing the haphazard terracing, shoddy fences of thorn-branches and the ankle-breaking sods, growing with every step more angry, and focussed, and righteous, and murderous.

At the river we spread into silent line abreast, filter through the trees, camouflaged, sweating, intent, containing our panting, slowing as we reach the open ground where the enemy awaits. Only two guerrillas are in sight now, hovering around a thatched grain-byre on the edge of the naked field. Thirsty, thirsting, we crouch, aim, I fire, and the others follow, volley rolling onto crackling volley of adrenaline and singing metal.

Both men go down. We stop firing, move quickly onto higher ground, wait. No sign of the other guerrillas. I report the contact. They will send a PRAW plane over. We wait. The two in the field are alive, prone, huddling against each other. Covering our flanks, we sweep through the treeline. Then Savuti and I approach them cautiously. I can feel my every step press against the earth, as if the earth itself were trembling flesh.

The younger of the two men has a cloth already wrapped tightly round a flesh wound in his upper arm. The older one, too old, lies on his back, groaning, his lower leg smashed, I guess beyond repair, by an MAG round. The mutilated limb oozes brilliant blood, shards of greased bone. All those rounds, only two hits.

'Who is your section commander?' I demand, with cunning subtlety.

The young man replies, acidly and in excellent English, 'I am not a terrorist, and I don't know anything about section commanders.'

Stumped, I examine their situpas. They appear to be in order. There are no weapons, no incriminating documents, anywhere in sight. 'Where are the other three men?'

'They are children, they have run away.'

I report back. I feel as if my chest is going to implode. I request a casevac for the wounded man. It is refused. The PRAW aircraft arrives and circles overhead. JohnWayne.

JohnWayne: One Alpha, confirm you've still got those wounded men with you?
One Alpha: Affirmative.
JohnWayne: Roger, ask them their names, where they live, and the name of their section commander.
One Alpha: Roger, the one's name is Zachabia Muneyi, and he lives at Mutenda, and he says he doesn't know anything about section commanders.
JohnWayne: Ja, it looks like you've bagged yourself a couple of civvies. Now I want you to bring this bloke back with you. Just keep him with you until you've completed your task, copied?
One Alpha: Roger, copied. What about the other one, he can't walk, over?
JohnWayne: Confirm he has deceased?
One Alpha: Negative, he's still alive.
JohnWayne: Confirm he has a head wound?
One Alpha: Negative, *leg* wound, copied?
JohnWayne: Confirm he could *get* a head wound?
(Pause.)
One Alpha: Ja, it could be arranged.
JohnWayne: Right, fine. I'm sure he could gap it and get shot, even with one leg.

The aircraft engine snarls and recedes into silence. I look down at the man. Black blood pulses in diminishing gouts from a severed artery. The sky reels in my head, the sunlight turning brittle and pale. I am afraid I am going to pass out. I pull the trigger, double-tap, the way we were trained, and turn away.

Savuti demands brusquely, 'Are we going to *help* this other one, too?'

'Leave him. We'll tell JohnWayne he escaped during the night.'

Cupping life and death in the palm of my hand.

Overnight, sleepless, listening to the others grunting and whispering through their dreams, I grapple afresh with my choices. In the first grim light of dawn, I write:

Last night the day's incident nagged at me, under the grey moon. It was not pretty, or even patriotic, it was ugly, futile, senseless. I tried Gallico's trick, thinking up stories 'until my mind rebels at doing overtime, goes numb, and I go to sleep'. But the stories I tell myself are themselves about the war, and my brain is inexorably tugged back to the horror of it all. To be sure, it is not to be avoided, to shut it away would mean the destruction of moral conscience, but still one has to harden the nerves to withstand it . . .

I keep thinking of Charlie Locker and Oscar Wilde, *It is not so much what we do that's evil, but what we become because of it.*

In the morning, as we hike up to higher ground, we look back across the valley. The man we left is still sitting next to the body of his friend. How will he move him? Who will he have to break the news to? I can hear women keening, somewhere in the future of my own heart.

We move on, burn down a few more huts, help ourselves to a couple of enamel plates. I set free some twenty gasping baby goats from a cramped and reeking pen. They reunite with their mothers in a cacophony of joyful bleats. Doubtless I will be cursed by the owners for this act of gratuitous kindness, too.

The Chungwe Valley opens out onto the scoured plains, like an outbreath of relief. The job is done. We radio in, wait for the trucks, keep vigilant at the roadside. There is always danger.

* * *

I miss Charlie Locker. I write to him.

How is Bullies? I'll see you in a few weeks, not much left of this crap to endure. We culled a probable gook in the Ch——, downed a couple of them as they ran. The wounded one was too young, I confess we let him go and lied to John Wayne that he slipped away from us when we were moving into gonk posi, and that we didn't want to compromise ourselves any further. I don't pray, but I hope you are praying I never have to go back there. Ever.

Knowing I am confessing through a tissue of half-truths and lies, I don't send the letter. But I fold it away into the back of a diary. As if accumulating evidence against myself.

In the days that follow, I reread the diaries I still have with me, trying to draw boundaries around my dishonesty. On the one hand, the truth is not entirely there, either. The diaries' evasiveness appals me. On the other hand, there are places where the written word proves conclusively that my memory has failed me, has refashioned itself into other fictions. Already I can feel the past sliding and rolling under my feet like oiled rocks in a streambed.

I bury the little black books in the bottom of my pack. I am tempted to burn them. I do not want to be the person they seem to say I am. I want to hole up, write nothing, say nothing. What is the point? The gap between the physical act and the imaginative act of writing seems unbridgeable, a curse. Is it possible that writing, literature, is *not* after all a civilising influence? Is it possible that it actually shields us from real life? I recall that Kommandants at Auschwitz or Belsen could go home and weep over Rilke's sonnets or Schubert sonatas. Art moved their souls in ways that their daily life of institutionalised murder did not. I doubt very much that I am as evil as Reinhard Heydrich or Rudolf Höss, but perhaps it is not so different.

So why should I write at all? I know, deep down, that no matter what despair I feel now, I cannot refuse myself the writing. I know, deep down, that I will go on writing, that I will pick up my pen again tomorrow, and for years to come, and indeed to the end of my days. *But for what?*

* * *

I write home:

> *Foul, despicable, degrading, this war. I am glad I will see little more of it, at least from this field angle. Will the medic be any less horrified by the things he sees? The machines man has made for his own destruction make one hell of a mess of that infinitely more beautiful, complex, vital machine, his body.*
>
> *No one is pleased with the war now. No one wants to go out again. No one, if they had their way, would do another stint, many say they will not anyway. And the Army aggravates it by little things like*

insisting on shaving off beards and wearing 'Army' flashes, things of which the men say, Well, if they're going to mess me around, I'll tell them I'm going . . . I have no doubt the other side and the poor people caught in the middle are as sick of it all as we are; this is a hope for a better turn.

For much of what's left of my time with F Company, I succumb to some violent gastric complaint. I lie on my stretcher, while the rest of the company takes on a task more daunting even than the Chungwe: clearing the Ngorima. Ngorima lies on the Mozambique border, a notorious 'liberated zone', silly with guerrillas, reputedly range-marked for mortars from one end to the other. A short-legged, redheaded farmer from Rusape takes over my stick. At the end of their first day, they are back, Redhead with a broken collar-bone.

'It was fuckin' unnerving,' Redhead babbles, laughing too much. 'We're making our way down this valley, right, and I'm squatting there checking out the map, when I hear this voice, "*Iwe, uya kuno!* Hey, you, come here!" And there's this great big gook sticking his head over the bushes, enormous bloody pot belly, all those Ngorima guavas, had a few myself, hey! He must have thought I was an Af, with all my camo paint and shit. So I whisper out the side of my mouth, I was frozen to the spot, man, my rifle round behind me somewhere, I sort of hiss at old Mbiti, "Hey, Mbiti, pull this cunt!" And Mbiti's got his face full of guava and says, "Who?" Then I just checked the gook's eyes go big, he was so close I could smell the dried shit on his arsehole, man! So I just took this header behind a tree and went down this great big bloody bank, dwang! I felt the old collar-bone snap. And old Mbiti wakes up and starts hammering away with his MAG, just spraying it all over the place and he nearly takes out Goldilocks on the ridge above us, hey!' And he whoops with laughter and then winces and clenches his face shut.

Two days later, the company suffers a much more serious engagement. They get stonked by mortars to hell and back. Tsoro acquires a cleanly-hollowed pink nick across the tip of his chin from a passing round. Mukwa, looking shocked and pasty, returns with grenade shrapnel in his chest and upper arms. *It should have been me collecting that shrapnel*, I think, and suffer once again that quivery sensation under the sternum, at once fulfilling and empty, of having had a narrow escape.

From my sickbed, I also monitor the progress of what is probably the most bizarre and ill-advised election in Rhodesia's history:

14 April. *On the phone Dad says we've killed 90 CTs today, and forces have gone into Lusaka to take out Nkomo's HQ and private home, and into Francistown to kidnap a couple of other ZIPRA big wheels. Great stuff. Dad seems to think there'll be a good turnout for the elections: most of the urban blacks will vote; the rurals are shaky.*

16 April. *Fresh companies have come in, ten-man sticks and almost all whites; they're running around in new, squat, vicious-looking Four-Five MAPs, very neat. Two polling booths have been hit already, one while moving in, the other in Manica TTL, one ES seriously wounded.*

17 April. *Go down to the fruit factory to vote. I put my cross against UANC, for what it's worth. Even the blacks have no idea what's going on, if not less. 'I'll see which is the prettiest picture,' says Gamara . . . Another polling booth was attacked and the 8RR defenders killed two and captured one CT. Someone said five or six Salisbury booths had been clobbered, no details. In the Ngorima, of a population of 20–30 000, a grand total of two have turned up to vote.*

Evening. The Ngorima total has gone up to 68. 1278 registered at the local booth, which is good. Not many, I suspect, had a hell of a lot of choice. I know a lot of farmers are taking their employees in to vote, whether they like it or not. On the news it says polling is brisk in the main centres; an estimated 20% have cast votes so far. Let's hope it picks up before dying down, in which case we should get our requisite 60% . . . There's been quite a bit of action around, an ambush and a landmine on the Chipinga convoy, 2 injured in the first, an already crippled girl killed in the second. 395 gooks have been killed since we came in . . . Some 60 base camps have been stonked in Hurricane and Thrasher, mostly SFA, Security Force Auxiliaries, no one killed in any of them. Salisbury Omnibus Co, Willowvale, got mortared, minor damage.

18 April. *Little has happened today. The news says 27% have voted*

*in the first two days. That's not so promising. Muzorewa is well in the
lead, so far. The sitreps say 100 trained guerrillas from Ethiopia were
landed at Beira, and are now heading for Enkeldoorn. Seems they're
Ndabaningi Sithole's men, probably to take out whoever's in power if
it isn't Sithole. Most of the whites have voted for 'Rubber Dinghy'
Sithole in the hope of affording Muzorewa some parliamentary op-
position and balance. A good thing as long as all parties maintain
democratic discipline, but if anyone's bent on violent overthrow it won't
help either way.*

*19 April. Escort some sticks to a local PV to vote. The voting is going
well, 47% now, it's very hopeful . . .*

*20 April. . . . We're fast running out of graze; all forces are supposed
to be on rat-packs for the election period, but we indented for extra
fresh rats beforehand. We're getting down to tins and compo packs
now, however.*
  They tell us we're demobbing on Monday 23rd.

*21 April. Camp greets us with long faces. We've been magnanimously
awarded another six days in the bush. Everyone had been prepared
for an extension, but not so late, not after being told that we were
demobbing in two days. Stupid, morale-damaging, unnecessary mistakes. The excuse is to provide a phased withdrawal after the
elections . . .*
  *Voting stood at 57,1% at 2 A.M. yesterday. Very, very good. Sev-
eral terrs have swapped sides in order to cast their votes, also a good
sign.*

A week or so later, I am less sanguine:

*The political scene is not rosy. The voting went well, 63,9%.
Muzorewa got in first by a long way. Which is fine except that Rubber
Dinghy Sithole is now very disgruntled and denouncing the election,
which he'd been supporting all along, as subject to 'gross irregularities',
wants to boycott Parliament, international commission, etc. Stupid,
power-hungry fool. This was predictable, of course; it is characteristic
of the black politician that he is more interested in himself than anyone*

*else. So we are poised on the brink of the biggest bloodbath in South-
ern African history. Civil war is very close, and we still have the other
war, except the white man is no longer in control, and no international
recognition forthcoming, not even from South Africa yet.*

And finally, on 4 May 1979, I write: 'Today 90 years of white rule end
with the dissolution of Parliament.' With that bald comment, there
seems to be nothing left to say.

* * *

Final confirmation of my place on the medics course comes through.
My father has planned an overseas trip for me once my National
Service is done. I have been accepted at university for the following
year. I feel the quickening pulsation of escape, of turning a corner, of
new leaves budding. At the same time, I suffer a sense of deadening,
a sense that nothing can really counterbalance, let alone eradicate,
the swarming violence I have found, like a nest of disturbed ter-
mites, infiltrating everything. I wonder if I can ever regain a sense of
faith in human nature. Or in my own.

My final act of obedience to my unit before I head for the medics
is to adorn the 4RR float, their civic contribution to Umtali's annual
spring parade. My father snaps a photo of me. There I stand, looking
absurdly burly, arms folded, in full camo, in front of a paper-flower-
bedecked Two-Five. The truck is surmounted by a lethal-looking
7-pounder howitzer – and two young girls in virginal white.

Along the side it proclaims in enormous letters: 'Make love, not
war.'

* * * * *

PART 4

New Leaves

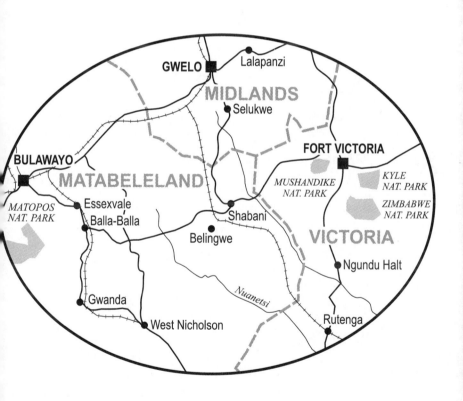

Chapter 9

Educating the Trout-Fly

On commence par tuer, on finit par guérir.

ONE BEGINS by killing, and ends by healing. Sitting on the grey blanket, the hubbub of the barrack-room around me, I decide to take these words of Van Gogh as a sign.

For the second time in two years, I find myself expending a birthday – this one my twentieth – in the numbing greyness of Llewellin Barracks. Its sprawling shabbiness closes round me like a raw fog. But inside myself I am exulting. I can hardly believe my good fortune, can hardly trace the sources of it. Was it cowardice impelled me here? A spiritual epiphany? Political foresight? Strangely, I can find no trace of my decision in the diaries. I seem to remember, intangible as a reflection on running water, Whorehound's florid face, the frog's mouth saying to me, 'Don't you want to be something more important than a skivvy, Arm? An officer? A driver? A medic?'

But I can't be sure I haven't made that memory up.

I do remember envying Brinjal, his earnest melancholy, his new-found enthusiasm as he headed off for his own medic's course. I mourn afresh his clumsy, catastrophic, unnecessary death. Maybe it began with him. Maybe I feel somehow I can replace him in the annals of compassion.

And I remember approaching Captain Apothecary at JOC Chipinga, long before I got shot at. Long before I killed. Less fearful than fed up, less compassionate than bored. But I can no longer sort out the mix of impulses. Perhaps it doesn't matter. I finger the seams of my same old camo shirt, worn pale with experience. I am still on the same side, part of the same machinery. If doing this course is a rebellion of sorts, it's incomplete, compromised, shadowy.

But the work is satisfying, deeply so. It feels like a transfusion of fruitful blood.

A sawing Glaswegian voice grates in my ear. 'What the fuck are yer readin' *noo*, Troot-Fly?'

They call me Trout-Fly because of my perky blue-and-white 4RR cockade.

'Van Gogh's letters to his brother,' I say.

'Van Fogarty, did ye say?' And he guffaws through his orange broomhandle moustache. Fogarty is an apelike, irascible, domineering Scot, a mercenary, a corporal in the SAS, endowed with all that unit's physical self-possession but none of its aristocratic affectations. He is insufferably loud, foully witty, hugely popular.

'Ye're a pompous little bloody book worrm, ye know that?'

I look him straight in his pale green eye. 'And you're an illiterate orang-utan, I suppose?'

'*Jee-sus!*' He appeals to the barrack at large. 'Did ye all hear what this little fookin' Foor-eyes just called me? I'll have ye charrged for insuboordination, ye wurrm. Fookin' Van Ghokxch, indeed,' he spits.

'It's pronounced "Van Goe",' says Parish.

'Ar, *jee-sus*, what have I doon to deserve all these intellecturrals, eh?'

Fogarty has done much to ease our conditions at the Medical Training School. The MTS itself lies half a kilometre or so outside Llewellin's main perimeter. This isolation already signifies some freedom from familiar constraints. Many of the trainees have their own vehicles; some live in Bulawayo and go home daily. Several are regulars or soldiers of fortune and are not amenable to being treated like rookies. Fogarty spearheads a regimen of systematic apathy in order to persuade early morning PT into retirement. He calls it his 'hor-r-rizontal campaign'. A further week into the course, a more energetic 'whinge parade' is launched. Fogarty, brandishing his orange-furred simian limbs, Glaswegian curses pouring from his undershot trap of a shark's mouth, gets us an upstairs room to ourselves in the graze-hall. We are granted relaxed living-out conditions. We have achieved a certain aristocracy. And we are housed in the superior NCO barracks – precisely those eight-bed units I temporarily haunted as a 'lizard' a year ago.

And every day, on my way to meals, just inside Llewellin's main gate and not far from that peeling basilica of a cinema, I pass the spot where Tractorback ran me down in his BMW Cheetah. I finger the callous of bone in my hand and thank the stars for that accident, without which I would not be here.

Lectures and weekly tests unfold with satisfying regularity. I can feel the flakes of rust sloughing from my brain. By now we have been whittled down by a series of exams and mishaps to forty or so. All but three of the blacks have been knocked out. 'Bloody right, too, what do you expect, mun.' How Hotbottle is still on the course at all is a mystery, since he has employed every imaginable device, from going AWOL to deliberately failing tests, to get himself off it. Panhandle, an RLI troopie, is in jail for beating up a girl who spurned his attentions at one of our numerous parties. Also in the slammer is a lean, serpentine solitary dubbed the Brain-Cell, who gruesomely murdered a taxi-driver near Norton or somewhere.

Naturally there are gentle, intelligent, and charming men on the course, too – not least of all the instructors, on the whole mild and inoffensive people. They are occasionally mean-spirited, but only because they are uncomfortable under the prickly mantle of authority. Warrant Officer Shovelly's languid threat, 'Beware the quiet man, for he hath fury', is received with derisive hoots. If many of us behave like recalcitrant schoolboys it is because, some terrible military experiences notwithstanding, that is what most of us still are.

I have purchased a textbook of anatomy and *Black's Medical Dictionary*, and fairly launch myself into studying the minutiae of the body. I find myself revelling in the miraculous creation that is the human being, its astonishing ecology of channels and nerves. I set out determined to be Best Student. It has soon become clear that this is a wildly inflated ambition. There are many clever people here. I've lowered my sights to Best Actor (we spend a great deal of time acting out casualty situations, sticking needles into, and frequently right through, one another's veins, and doctoring a variety of potentially fatal 'wounds').

Now Fogarty offers a parting shot. 'I hope ye fail tomorrer's test, ye ponce, same as the last one!'

'I got 82 percent, actually.'

'Well, 82 per*cent*, Troot-Fly!' He rolls his eyes heavenwards. 'An' there was I all along thinkin' ye were a bit slow, like – a rreal *thick-shit!*'

* * *

Body systems; the cell; types of cell; organisation and types of tissue; bones and muscles; blood, blood vessels, blood pressure; blood composition; the kidney; acid balance; pharmacology; respiratory system; intramuscular injections; hospital administration; suturing; urine testing; the eye, the nose, the skin, the tongue; endocrine system; bacteriology; IVI; medical forms; bandaging; digestive system; first aid; asphyxia; cardiac arrest; artificial resuscitation; haemorrhage; ambulance drills; fractures, burns, gunshot wounds; shock; ballistics; allergies; concussion and compression; chest drains; trauma to ear and eye; spinal systems; antibiotics; ENT infections; analgesics; otitis media; poultices; inhalations; abdominal trauma; casevac priorities; stores management forms; head and hand injuries; strains, sprains and dislocations; nausea and vomiting; appendicitis; peritonitis; ulcers; antacids; antispasmodics; diarrhoea, constipation, anti-diarrhoeals; Sick Parades; food poisoning; gastric enteritis; haemorrhoids; ointments and creams; face injuries; trypanosomiasis; rabies; plaster casts; tetanus; scabies, dermatitis and eczema; tickbite fevers; lice; tinea; blisters; hyperidosis; metatarsalalgia; nutrition; blood disorders; bilharzia; STDs; intubation; catheterisation; first-aid lecture techniques; drug interactions; sewerage; camp hygiene; boils and carbuncles; emergency childbirth; public health; asthma; ingrown toenails; heat exhaustion; epileptic fits; veld sores; dermatitis, neuro-dermatitis and hives; migraines; anti-inflammatories, antiemetics and antiseptics; road traffic accidents; malaria; cholera; chest injuries; pneumonia; snake bite.

Disposal of the dead.

* * *

Vincent van Gogh wrote to his brother:

There may be a great fire in our soul, but no one ever comes to warm himself at it, and the passers-by see only a little smoke coming through the chimney, and pass on their way.

As usual I am slow to find soulmates. I spend the first few weekends of the course relaxing at the venerable Macdonald's servicemen's Club in downtown Bulawayo. I prowl the city's small bookshops. I pursue a solitary appraisal of the Bulawayo Trade Fair, which I consider 'not up to much, though even a local might be surprised at the extent of Rhodesian manufacture and self-sufficiency'. I get most satisfaction from the Chipangali Wildlife Orphanage's display of genets and leopard. It reminds me of home and of Mana Pools, that other life within this life.

I decline to go pub-crawling with my fellow-trainees, so avoid the scraps that regularly erupt in the Beer Garden between whites and blacks, with the police getting bottled in between. The whites are usually arrested, the blacks simply shepherded away. That is the way the country is going, it seems.

Fortunately, other avenues are open to fulfil my desires for companionship. The Jeek, erstwhile school antagonist and friend, has been posted to Bulawayo. He is now a cop, a fully-fledged 'Beebarp'. He is as insufferably and generously Christian as ever. Through him I meet numerous golden-hearted people with whom I can spend deliciously humane moments of non-militarised time. The Jeek, despite his devotion to the church, reveals a quite predatory persistence in the pursuit of women. His rounded face focussed as a gun barrel, he drags me around with him to aid his dogged wooing of a pudgy but winning young chemist. She lives in the posh, mellow suburb of Hillside. Between long, drowning kisses on the sitting-room couch, they test me on my medical knowledge.

For me, too, the lust for female companionship, and a woolly musing about the possibilities of spiritual enlightenment, become inextricably tangled. I agonise over the heartfelt but unwanted attentions of an old school girlfriend. At the same time I find myself entertaining quivery feelings about a Salisbury trainee teacher I meet on R&R. She and I exchange a few letters. She characterises mine as 'cleverly ambiguous', divines me for a 'romantic fool', and brings the thing to an end.

And there is the lure of women in The Jeek's more accessible church circle.

The first time The Jeek invites me to church, I sit uncomfortably through a stifling sermon and the unctuous greetings of strangers recognising a bemused interloper. I find the platitudes plastic, the hymns hollow. The 'prayers for the boys on the border', sincere but colourless, make me feel singled out and prickly around the nape. I do enjoy the vivacious singing of an evangelistic youth group who style themselves, in the odd manner of such 'warriors for Christ', S.M.I.T.E. The gulf between their kind of warfare and mine is underlined when, with naïve temerity, they visit Llewellin Barracks. They scatter themselves amongst the troops one lunch-time. Their demure and long-toothed lead singer sits down at my table. My heart goes out to her when Severance, an RLI troopie of pitted face and incorrigibly tactless disposition, grates out loudly, 'Okay, which of you fuckin' pagan wankers is gunna say Grace, then?'

I go to one of The Jeek's Bible-study groups. I huddle in an arm-chair and a confusion of feelings, wondering why I have come. The subject is the role of the High Priest in the Old Testament.

> *I find this fascinating, though as always I feel they read too much into the Biblical words and events; the cynic in me doesn't let me regard it as more than a fallible historical document. They think I am a full Christian, and I don't have the heart to disillusion them. I even lie a little. Hypocrite. Yet I feel easier in these Christians' wonderful company than in any other – they are so clean-scrubbed, earnest, giving.*

And when things seem particularly to be going organisationally awry, I write: 'Lord's will be done.' Then, surprised at myself, I add:

> *I seem to be saying that to myself more and more often: It's the Lord's will; Thank the Lord. Why? Am I becoming a Christian, half-unwilling? Destiny or propaganda? If it is propaganda, I've deliberately subjected myself to it. Why do I go to church? I have pride in my willpower to refuse to do something I'm not going to enjoy. Is it a need for God's love? Or people's love? Are they the same thing?*

I suspect myself of being driven more by loneliness than by a new metaphysical awareness. Church becomes more interesting when I meet Tanathe. A hotel receptionist, she is too tall for me, clear-skinned, and none too bright. But there is something elevating and graceful about her vapid and dark-eyed vivacity. We sit together in church a few times, touch in momentary cool fevers under Bulawayo's ubiquitous jacaranda trees. The Jeek notices, of course, and asks slyly:

'You got a little thing going with Tan'?'

Shrug. 'Ya, well . . .'.

'You quite fond of her?'

'Yeah, she's nice.'

'You know, I've never seen you blushing before, Dan.'

'When was I blushing?' prickly.

'You're blushing *now*.'

Tanathe and I finally have supper together at her tiny flat, neither of us knowing to wait for the water to boil before putting the spaghetti in. The glutinous meal complete, we sit, hold hands, murmur, tentatively kiss. An erection bulbing interestingly in the cramped quarters of my shorts, I lean and nuzzle her pale neck, dark curls tickling the bridge of my nose, and whisper admiringly, 'Your skin is so *soft*.'

'Oh for heaven's sake!' she snaps, 'That's such a cheap line!'

And that, pretty much, is that.

But there is also a wider, even more unbridgeable gap between us: I simply cannot reconcile her rather winsome and idealistic Christian belief and her all-loving God, with the vicious scents of gun-oil and cordite, the raucous evils which we ourselves are meting out daily. The violence I know clouds the blood in my own veins.

I talk to Charlie Locker. It takes me three weeks to contact him. I am afraid he will somehow be ashamed of me. But the stiffness of our last days in Chipinga has evaporated. He envelops me in his bony arms, takes me home, tells his kids that I am their long-lost brother. He unpeels the clenched heart of my reticence, petal by petal. I tell him things I have not been able to tell my own father. He absorbs it all like a dark pool, closes over it, unruffled. No one I have ever known is so adept at simply being *in* the moment. I don't know if I can ever achieve such equanimity against the past.

'So what's the problem with going to church?' he asks.

'I just feel so bad. I know I'm being a hypocrite. It *is* kind of beautiful, you know? I just can't make sense of it, though. If they knew what I'd done . . .'.

'Would they reject you? Is that what you're afraid of?'

'I think I'm more afraid they'd fall over me trying to exorcise the Devil from my heart! I would be the most imperfect person amongst them. It just doesn't make sense, though. It seems to me they're saying, Okay, we're imperfect, so we must have fallen from perfection, Eden or whatever; therefore there must be a perfect God. I don't know about that logic.'

'Hm. The problem of evil. All the theologians have grappled with that one. Augustine. Anselm. Küng. Something like, If God is perfectly good, he must *want* to abolish all evil. If he is unlimitedly powerful, he must be *able* to abolish all evil. But clearly he has done neither. Therefore, either God is not perfectly good, or he is not limitlessly powerful.'

And I sit there, hands between my knees, stunned by the simple insuperability of that formulation. I cannot get beyond the sound of the double-tap shot, my own inability to look at what I had done.

And I cannot call myself evil, either. I am here because I want to save lives, I tell myself. I can only be evil if I committed murder, if murder it was, by my own free will. That is what the Christians always say. God gave us free will. I know I chose to pull that trigger. Yet I do not *feel* I chose.

* * *

Becoming a medic doesn't distance one from the brutality. It brings it closer.

The School prepares us as intensively and thoroughly as anyone could expect in the short time available. In between lectures and tests, we inflict numerous dramas of imaginary trauma on one another, sometimes in places of unnecessary remoteness. One such exercise involves a mass deployment out to Essexvale to stage a 'multiple-casualty landmine-and-ambush scene'. Of course we 'medics' have to wade through a frigid river to reach the site. I am uncomfortably reminded of those COIN exercises in basic training. But now I know how to survive this. I am beginning to feel I can survive almost anything.

At the site there are theatrically writhing bodies everywhere. We rush from one casualty to another. Procedures are becoming automatic, smooth, almost beautiful. Spunky Mac MacGall plays the hysteric, whimpering misleading advice and tangling his feet in the drip tubes and running off into the koppies. He does it so well a scowling Fogarty has to run after him for an hour and a half and drag him back by the scruff.

I know in that moment that I have lost the Best Actor prize, too.

We begin to spend nights on duty at Mpilo General Hospital. These are very real, and much less fun. Mpilo is an austere labyrinth of yellowing aspect and echoing corridors. It is reserved for blacks. We novices are permitted to practise on blacks until we drop. Weekends and paydays produce welters of stab-wounds, axe gashes, bruised babies and broken noses, and the aftermath of drunken vehicle accidents. We hone our suturing skills with real Korean nylon, mop up real blood with stinging acriflavine, and squeeze real antibiotics into the upper-outer-quadrants of genuinely needy buttocks. These nights spill into the wee hours.

One or two patients die beneath our gaze. For some, clearly, civilian life is as tenuous, dangerous, bloodied, as anything I have encountered in the bush.

We visit an ailing haemophiliac, listen through a stethescope to the soughing lungs of a pneumonia victim, and participate in a pelvic examination on a large woman with a bellyache. I wonder how she feels; even here we wear our camouflage uniforms, surely the darkest symbol of her oppression. And here I am, peering curiously through the speculum at the reddened wall of her very womb, while my partner Snitchum explodes, 'Fuck that, you won't catch *me* sniffing up some kaffir bitch's cunt.'

I smile down at her and press her hand. But there is no response.

The final act is more real yet. The military pressures in the whole country are intensifying. The elections, of course, have solved nothing. We are needed, inexperienced as we are. Instead of a final, week-long practical at Essexvale, we are crash-deployed into the operational areas. Ten of us, our forearms patched with telltale haematomas of varying hue, like parodic stigmata, are sent to the south-east. We will be based with 9 RAR at Fort Victoria, and on 24 July rumble out there via Balla Balla, Filabusi, Shabani, Mashaba.

The country is looking grey and fleshless with winter, fire-charred in purgatorial swathes.

The RAR barracks sprawl, acres of red-brick flats seething with black people. We feel we might legitimately greet another white man with 'Dr Livingstone, I presume.' At the infirmary, an apparently boneless ragdoll of a Sergeant-Major with a sly smile and a thyroid condition fixes us with one bulging blue eye and rasps: 'I hope you buggers learned something at med school – you're going to need it. And don't expect to cuff it – you'll be walking three hours into base, digging fire-trenches, getting mortared etcetera etcetera. Our usual tactic nowadays is to deploy four-man sticks into open areas with a mock stretcher case. To draw fire, you understand.' Then the prominent eyes disappear surprisingly into crows'-feet. 'You'd better come in and get your packs.'

The medic-packs are awkward fold-out canvas affairs, scantily equipped with syringes and forceps, drips and bandages, scissors and sutures, a couple of vials of morphine, some Stemetil, some Crystapen. We supplement this meagre supply with bits and pieces filched from the stores at the Fort Vic hospital. Then wait. We make beds and dress wounds in the fenced-off military ward, where security forces, guerrillas, and doubtfuls-in-between are all treated holus-bolus.

'Pamper those gooks with a clean set of sheets and some Mazoe orange squash,' boasts the chapped-looking nurse in charge, 'and they're fully "on side". Just like that.'

And through the narrow doors of a mobile surgical theatre we glimpse an amputation. They are quick to amputate here, especially if the injured is a black person. It's cheaper. The bloody stump of the victim's leg glows against the green sheets like the end of a burning log.

Shabby Fort Vic has little to offer us. I am not displeased to get back to the bush.

So I find myself crammed shoulder-to-shoulder with four sticks of half-asleep RAR troops in the chilling coffin of a MAP, rumbling through the night into the fearsomely rocky heart of Chibi TTL. There, the int. has it, at least 150 guerrillas await our attentions with bated breath. I am conscious of being quite seriously underprepared, with inadequate warm clothing, my Swiss Army knife forgotten at home, my webbing coming apart after months of punishment, the medic's pack strapped cumbersomely over the top, and only five days' rations for an eight-day patrol.

Even the thin cutting of moon has slipped off the end of the world by the time they drop the last seven of us off on an anonymous roadside. Crickets' songs fill the dark. We are led by a terrifyingly burly, solicitous, competent Ndebele sergeant-major I think of as The Bulldog. These black soldiers are seasoned by years of fighting. I am the only white man, and the most junior, the tyro in every prickling pore. It is a salutory, discomfiting, liberating reversal of roles.

The thinnest milk of starlight lights our way as we make good progress through scented, rasping grassland – until our MAG gunner, ahead of me and slightly to one side, abruptly disappears, with scarcely a sound.

I grope forward, hissing to the others to halt. A gaping hole yawns beneath my hands. An old pit trap, probably. I can just make out the top of the gunner's head moving sluggishly below me.

'Are you hurt?'

He can manage no more than a muffled grunt, it seems. I strip my gear and slide down into the hole beside him. It seems to be his ankle, sprained at least, maybe broken.

We are halfway to hauling him out by his webbing when there's a sharp warning hiss, and an outburst of automatic fire. Muzzle flashes and jagged red tracers punch away into the dark; flailing limbs crunch us back into the hole. Trying to keep my head below the rim I grope through the grass for my rifle, can't locate it, for a moment enact in reality those horrible dreams that sometimes surface, in which I suddenly find myself without my weapon, can't recall where that constant companion is, can feel the panic rising.

Two men running, apparently. We fan out defensively, wait. The multiple skirl of crickets resumes. There is no return fire.

With the gunner down, and having well and truly compromised our position, we have little choice but to heft and piggyback the injured man back to the road, wait, and radio for a casevac in the morning. I feed him a couple of Doxypol to dull the pain, and we settle into a shallow bush-covered depression alongside the road. Cold and restless, we push guard in pairs for an hour at a time.

Somewhere far in the distance, mortars crump. The sly Ragdoll wasn't so far from the truth after all.

And at some point in the night, I feel a hard, tense hand close warningly around my bicep. I listen, my throat locked in dryness, to the soft padding of many feet along the invisible road just metres in front of us. It has to be guerrillas, maybe twenty. Nobody moves.

In the morning, we spend several hours trying to raise a casevac, and eventually have to hitch our way through to Rutenga. The Bulldog treats me like a son, buying me drink after drink, cooking for me, pointing out roots I might trip over when we walk around the bleak, mopani-fringed airstrip talking life and military tactics. He manages all this without the slightest loss of rank or dignity, is intelligent, generous, sharply witty, and utterly himself. In the diary, I judge him 'one of the finest blacks I've ever met – maybe one of the finest *men*'.

My sole duty in life, The Bulldog informs me as he leaves to join the local Fire Force, is to minister to the taciturn Broken-Foot. We truck the latter off to the hospital at Nuanetsi, and return to Rutenga without him. With nothing better to do, I wander into the MI room to see if I can lend a hand.

'Shit, I must be popular!' glares the medic there, 'you're the third blimmin' rookie to say that this morning!' Two of my fellow-trainees, the absurdly red-headed Tracer and his inseparable sidekick, an exuberant Brit named Pacer, have just been sent over to back up the Fire Force Starlight. Tracer'n'Pacer have spent an icy couple of nights on a koppie crest waiting in vain to nab some cattle rustlers. 'I thought we were supposed to be *medics*, not bloody shepherds!'

The Fire Force Starlight is a dapper little Indian named Khan.

'Well, you aren't medics yet. I got five years experience at this, you'll never catch me up. But you know what, I'm still a blimmin' lance-corp. My boss, he's an MA2, I'm an MA3, he's a national serviceman, I'm a regular. But him, he's a sergeant already. One guess why.' And he points at the dark skin of his right cheek. 'You guys, you'll be sergeants too in six months. Well, I say good luck to you. End of the year, I'm off to India.'

The Fire Force itself is just churning in out of the bleached winter sky: several Alouettes, a portly Dakota, a snarling Lynx. They are throwing every man-jack into the Chibi operation, since the CTs have been getting particularly adept at disrupting the heavy rail traffic coming through Rutenga from South Africa: long trains of sanctions-busting fuel trucks. Khan, with grim enthusiasm, tells us about the little five-man armoured trolley that patrols 100 k's of railway every night. Just a fortnight ago, it detonated a 'party-pack' of six landmines, was completely thrown over; the occupants, strapped in, were quite unhurt, 'but their lug-holes sang like cathedral bells, I tell you what!'

I find myself at the eye of a small, sporadic storm. I am content to let Tracer'n'Pacer hurtle off into the jaws of death with the Fire Force sticks. With only two-and-a-half weeks of my entire National Service to go, I have no further desire to place myself in the path of an AK round. Instead, I spend the days administering VD injections and dabbing mercurochrome on the fist-battered lips of local railwaymen, while the Fire Force choppers rage back and forth. I remember guarding the fuel that time above the Chungwe Valley, while the battle drummed invisibly below the skyline. It's inglorious, but safe.

Tracer'n'Pacer bring in their first casualty, a shrapnel nick in a soldier's ear. He was on one of the OP sticks that were deployed alongside The Bulldog's that night, and they have just survived being mortared for three-and-a-half hours. They started firing back, but it was a waste of ammo in the dark. They just had to sit it out amongst the reverberating rocks, while the guerrillas yelled inventive insults out of the night and preceded each shell with 'Watch *this* one!'

The hondo continues over the following days. All but one of the OPs are getting stonked. Mac MacGall's stick is flown in, Mac himself looking yellow and haggard.

'Jesus, we were revved for six hours. They've got all the artillery in the world out there, I can tell you. Then, we're coming off our gomo, and we run smack into about a dozen gooks, whadda-whadda. Culled two of 'em, but Christ, I never want to have to live through that again. Not ever.'

Then our time is up and we trundle back to Fort Victoria, over the mopani-scrub tableland pimpled with startled koppies, and through Ngundu Halt's community of domes, naked elephantine granite, streaked with black like old blood, or tears.

* * *

The medics' course draws to a close in a clutter of fussy details, dis-organisation, ironic juxtapositions. We have straggled back into the School with a variety of tales of excitement and ennui. Our only casualty is Don Ferrenzy, who got hit in the ankle when the Salisbury–Bulawayo train was ambushed near Selous. I am grilled by the CID over the disappearance of the hifi from Macdonald's Club. Lectures, practicals, and 'lecturettes' we each have to give on per-sonal research topics (mine, perhaps appropriately, on the dangers of alcohol), grind on. We are dragooned into guard duty over Mar-ried Quarters. Sergeant Dominy gets knocked down to private for being drunk on duty. Buddy Oldwalk, a pleasant graduate of the University of Cape Town, deservedly gets the extravagantly-sized Winthrop Shield for Best Student. Mac MacGall, as we have all anticipated, gets Best Actor.

Proud as Boy Scouts getting Bronze Arrows for long-jump, we buy and don our red-blue-and-yellow stable-belts and our corporal's stripes, ready for the final journey out, Starlights all.

In a fit of misguided hopefulness, I revisit Tanathe. She is open and charmingly forgiving, but when I invite her to our end-of-course dance, she replies in a note, execrably typed. There are no hard feelings, she writes, but I am interfering with her 'Christian life'. The last time I see her is sitting ahead of me in church, tucking her cheek into her shoulder in that devastatingly coy way she has. I long to reach forward and touch the bared curve of her elegant neck.

She does not say goodbye.

I resort as usual to brooding into the plashing complexities of the Centenary Park fountain. Rather than admit that I am simply soci-ally inept, I couch the problem in a Yeats-like argument between Soul and Body:

> Soul took Body's hand
> And they walked out into the night.
> Silently they wrestled it out
> Under a spire of dancing water.

In that poem, Soul and Body end in a 'truce'.

'That sounds to me like wishful thinking,' says Charlie Locker gently. 'Are you undergoing a crisis of belief still?'

'Just a little one.' I smile.

'There are no *little* crises of belief, my friend. Belief is always everything.'

We are saying goodbye in a town café. He doesn't want to embarrass me, and sticks out his angular hand.

'No, I want a hug. I'm trying to learn to express my true feelings.' He laughs delightedly. 'Will I see you again, Charlie?'

He looks me straight in the eye, the drooping eyelid doesn't twitch. 'You know you will. But don't forget, *There is always danger*.'

And The Jeek squeezes my shoulder in farewell, outside his church. 'You don't know how glad I am to see you learning to believe in the Lord,' he says, only slightly unctuously.

But I have to be honest with him: 'Jeek, I don't even know what is meant by "believe", yet.'

He doesn't hesitate. 'Me neither, sometimes. It's a long road.'

As we clear from MTS in a paroxysm of unnaturally friendly handshakes, and my National Service comes at long last to its close, I am clearly on the threshold of a new life. The very sky seems to pulse with it. As Van Gogh had also written, '*Il y a du bon en tout mouvement*'.

There is good to be found in all movement.

* * *

Going home to my parents, to their mountain retreat, is to re-enter that long-cherished civilian life. But it is in no way to escape the war. Like every other rural landowner, my mother goes around with a .38 Special strapped to her hip and drives with a Sten gun on the car seat. Her self-sacrificial devotion to animals remains unchecked. She pursues a finely-tuned speciality which is probably unique to the continent, if not the planet. This involves spending days on end alone in the hills with her tracker-dog, searching for lost pets. She usually finds them caught up in poachers' wire snares. Time and again my father and I sit in a worried silence on our veranda, as dusk falls, and she has not returned, and we begin to wonder if we can expect her home at all, or if we will learn too late that she has been shot by guerrillas, or been blown up by an antipersonnel mine, or simply fallen off a cliff.

She also takes it upon herself to rescue animals left behind by the increasingly frequent farm murders. On my second day home, she hears about two octogenarian brothers from Imbeza Valley. We used to live there, they were old friends, kindly innocuous men with tweeds and pipes. They have been murdered in their sleep by guerrillas. No one can tell her what has happened to the brothers' Labrador. Against the express orders of the military, out she goes. We wait. In the afternoon she returns. She found the dog still cowering under the bed, his coat black with the blood that had soaked through the mattress.

The elderly are particularly vulnerable to these cowardly and merely terroristic attacks. Three days later, the Agric-Alert yammers, a reaction stick is needed. Gunfire has been heard from a neighbour's place, the siren is going. I have finished my National Service, but I still have my Army FN. I join the stick, six of us in Rick Gongworthy's Land-Rover. The place seems deserted. As we enter the house we can smell the cordite. Smashed glass and furniture. The siren yowling. For a while we do not hear the whimpering.

Rick Gongworthy calls out, 'George! Jean?'

Jean has locked herself in the bathroom. There are bullet-holes splintering the catch. She is unhurt, white, gibbering, keeps saying, 'I'm sorry, I wet myself, I wet myself, George, George? I wet myself.'

George is dead. He was mending the roof, was gunned down without warning, lies crumpled up beneath the eaves, his head grotesquely crooked beneath his shoulder. We straighten him out a little, cover him, wait for the ambulance, the Army and the trackers.

'Jesus,' says my father. 'He was 71, built this place with his own hands, what harm did he ever do to those bastards?'

'Not a pretty sight,' Rick Gongworthy keeps muttering with grim vehemence, 'not a pretty sight,' like something he has learned from a movie.

Then my mother is out there, two days running, looking for the Persian cat and a sulphur-crested cockatoo. The cockatoo, when finally rescued, can't stop saying, 'Hello! . . . hello! . . . hello! . . . hello! . . .'.

Why our own house is never attacked is a mystery. It is so vulnerable, backed into the forest, into which attackers could melt almost without trace. We have grenade-screens over the bedroom windows, and twin halogen security lamps at each of the house's four corners, but the great forest milkwoods come so close to the walls that the lights do little but cast even denser shadows. We never put up the ten-foot security fences favoured by most farmers. We rely on the hypersensitive dogs, and signs from the wildlife itself, to warn us of intruders.

The only time we come close to getting hit is when the houses at the bottom of the valley get stonked from across the border, and a stray round clips through the trees above our roof. The dogs almost seem to hear it coming, instantly race out barking and run the offending missile off the property. The dogs are also highly effective in chasing off intruding helicopters and spotter-planes, which are a disturbance to the Sanctuary no matter whose side they're on.

'Those dogs know the story,' my mother avers. 'They know that it's always the ecology that really gets hammered in a war. No one thinks of it, until afterwards they look, and almost every human being is still alive, but all the fields are black and the forests full of mines that blow up the poor damned animals.'

After our elderly neighbour's murder, tensions are running particularly high. A couple of attacks have even been launched on Umtali town itself, which we can see, eight k's away across the ridges, from our upstairs veranda. Once, awakened in the small hours by mortar fire and responding artillery, we made some tea and watched the tracers flying entertainingly back and forth across the dark backdrop of the hills. The only casualties of these rather desultory and amateurish attacks have been a few holes in the golf course, damage to the Police pub (which certain Army hoipoloi considered An Excellent Thing), and the demolition of one cherished vintage car.

Nor are there any human casualties during two attacks on Dangamvura, one of Umtali's African townships.

'I can't for the life of me understand why the gooks are shelling their own people,' says my father.

'Oh, it must be the Selous Scouts. They do *all* the nasty things.'

'If it were them I'd at least expect them to do a decent job of it. These so-called freedom fighters are completely useless. How the hell have we managed to lose the war to them?'

'But they still kill people. Us. And Rick says some were sighted not far from the Burma turn-off yesterday.'

In this charged atmosphere, a meeting of our valley's Defence

Committee is convened at the local hotel. We have acquired a resident militia now, a group of Guard Force blacks led by a wiry, intense Belgian. This mercenary has a quick-footed gait, and an undershot jaw pale with blond bristle. Everyone calls him CaneRat. CaneRat is now threatening to resign because his Guard Force personnel are such a 'shower of sheety'. (I can see, looking around the withdrawn faces, that some would welcome his departure this very minute, since they disapprove of an advert he placed in the *Umtali Post* for a 'gewgaw girl' – and they disapprove even more of the pretty little blonde piece who answered it.) Bucknall-Squires, banana-farmer and resident officer for Guard Force, bridles at CaneRat's calumnies. Jabbman suggests reducing the militia force to two whites (expensive because – obviously – they have to be paid more than the blacks) and eight Guard Force men. There should be two sticks, one static, one mobile. The women should be employed more fully for the paperwork and radio watch, freeing up their husbands to patrol and man roadblocks.

'Not a damn, I'm staying home at night to protect my family.'

'No, sure, I'm only talking about daytime ops.'

'Tell me, why is Umtali Rural Police being run by a bloody eighteen-year-old?'

'I think Ritchie's doing a damn good job.'

'I'm not saying he isn't – for an eighteen-year-old.'

'Look, let's get practical – all the terrs are coming in from the TTL, so at the very least we should blitz a kind of cordon san, sanit-whatever – a no man's land –'

'With booby traps.'

'Agent Orange.'

'Ag, just nuke the whole TTL, mun.'

'Maybe we should at least clear the roadsides, say twenny feet or so, make ambushes harder –'

'Jesus, Jim, on all those bends –'

'But no one's ever been ambushed on that road, so why –'

'And the floppies'll just ambush from twenty feet further back, that's all.'

'Well, we know the bastards can't shoot straight unless they're less than *ten* feet away –'

'No, I think it's basically a good idea, but who's gonna *do* all this clearing?'

'Can we borrow that munt of yours with his chainsaw, Bob? He'll be through by 1998!'

'And how the hell do we finance this lot? Quite a few people in this valley, who shall remain nameless, haven't paid their dues for *last* year yet.'

'Well, I'll tell you quite frankly, I'm not forking out any more clams for this Farm Protection Unit thing, I don't have a shred of evidence yet that it even *exists* –'

'Now hang on a bit, John –'

The meeting threatens to deteriorate into barely-veiled recriminations over past abuses and omissions. Rick Gongworthy, smooth as a lawyer and looking as if he is about to burst out of his scarlet skin like an overheated sausage, sums up the suggestions and implications and sends us all away to think about them. The air has not been one of panic, rather of electric concern blunting apparently arrogant confidence. A kind of pragmatic gravity underpins the banter. Above all, the sense of besiegement is intense.

It is more or less under the pigeon-toed and silver-tongued Gongworthy, in command more by virtue of eloquence than experience, that a final comic-opera foray is conducted. This event confirms my view that the war has reached its nadir of stupidity. Two days before I am due to fly out to Johannesburg and London on my long-promised trip, we are interrupted at our suppers by a furious outbreak of automatic fire from the vicinity of the militia base. I think I can hear RPD fire. My father thinks it might be the Roads Camp getting revved. The Agric-Alert radio snaps and yowls. A reaction stick, seven or eight of us dressed in a motley of Police Reserve blue, Army camo, and anything else dark and warm that leaps to hand, assemble at Gongworthy's turn-off. Our job is to walk a few hundred metres into an ambush posi on the junction with the main Vumba road, west of the militia's farmhouse base and the adjacent Road Camp.

We set off along the valley road: *Hsst, spread out for Chrissake!* Jabbman's boots squeak alarmingly in the magnifying dark. Effortsen drops an FN magazine and has to scrabble about in the grass verge for scattered rounds. Huge Afrikaner van Rensburg can't keep his voice below a boom resonant as a ground hornbill. Gongworthy's walkie-talkie burbles and hisses like water in a tin drainpipe. Long before we get there, the firing has stopped. A vehicle sweeps towards us along the road. We stand transfixed like rabbits in its headlights until it passes: one of those hybrid paramilitary Land-Rovers the Rhodesians are so adept at inventing, bristling with armaments and patched with sandy camo and looking like a four-wheeled poisonous angelfish. It neither fires on us, nor stops.

We reach the junction with the main road. 'Okay, mate, you're probably the best shot, you get on top of that bank on the other side . . .'.

'Are you crazy, we'll pull each other, we must all be on the same side . . .'.

'Ah, right.'

We slosh across the muddy ditch and crunch about on broad dry muzhanje leaves looking for some meagre cover. Hunkered down in the darkness, we wait.

Nothing happens. An Army truck thunders down the road and turns in at the militia base. Nothing further. We can raise no one on the walkie-talkie now. So we toddle on down to the base in a cautiously sheepish gaggle to find out what is going on. CaneRat is scampering about excitedly rearming his men. His blonde gewgaw is taping over a leaking hole in a sandbag. Has anyone been hit? No. The Roads Camp fellow is yammering into the radio. They fired on some movement beyond their perimeter and then all hell broke loose, he says. No, they don't have any casualties, either. Has anyone seen green AK tracer? Um, no, funnily enough, they don't think so.

It gradually becomes clear just what has happened. Gongworthy's belly wobbles above his webbing belt with irascible disbelief.

'You *arseholes!* You and the Roads Camp have been shooting at *each other!*'

* * *

My green rucksack is packed. It is my last day at home.

I do not feel, as T.E. Lawrence did when he left the RAF, like a 'lost dog'. On the contrary. But my exhilaration at leaving the military is tempered by distress. I do not want to leave our mountain paradise. I haven't been to many other countries, so I have no evidence for it, but I am inwardly convinced that this is still one of the most beautiful places on Earth. I am also distressed that I am abandoning my parents just when security is most tenuous.

Not that all is entirely well overseas: I have noted in my diary that the 79-year-old Lord Mountbatten has just been blown to pieces in his yacht off Sligo. Both the IRA and the Irish National Liberation Army have leapt, with grotesque alacrity, to claim responsibility. At least one of them has to be both mad and untruthful. I condemn them as no better than our own CTs, and heartily agree with Lawrence, who wrote exactly 50 years before:

I think the planet is in a damnable condition, which no change of party, or social reform, will do more than palliate insignificantly. What is wanted is a new master species – birth control for us, to end the human race in fifty years – and then a clear field for some cleaner mammal. I suppose it must be a mammal?

I have never wanted to end the human race entirely, but I am certainly dubious about our own 'change of party', from a white to a black government.

2 September 1979. My last day at home. I write:

The new black-red-white-green flag of Zimbabwe-Rhodesia – it will be Zimbabwe soon – was raised in all major centres at eleven o'clock this morning. Herald of change. What will it be like when I return? Red for blood, or green for prosperity? I say I love this country, but how do I know until it is lost? I will know when I see the Limpopo recede beneath the wing.

On the following day, on my way to the outward-bound bus, I hand in my familiar old FN rifle, my *vade mecum* of so many months, and walk out of Brigade Headquarters feeling vulnerable and bereft. Technically, I owe the Army one more call-up. As I stride off under the jacarandas, I silently exult: *They will not get me.*

My rucksack stowed on the bus, my father shakes my hand, firm and formal as always.

'Don't you dare come back,' he warns. 'I haven't paid your way overseas to have you coming back into this nonsense.' That is how he expresses his care, it's the way he is. I feel a huge surge of gratitude, somehow can't say it. I know that I will be leaving him behind in more ways than one.

Then he shakes my hand briskly again and sees me safely onto the bus for Salisbury, the airport, and the world. It is 3 September – the fortieth anniversary of the start of another, much greater war, and the end of my much littler one. As the bus moves off, my father raises his big red fist in salute, and I raise my slighter one in reply. Umtali town, an impressionist canvas in mauve jacaranda and scarlet flamboyant blossoms, slides away behind the granite complex of Murahwa's Hill. From the topmost curve of Christmas Pass I take in a last, gulping glance at the far green wave of Zohwe ridge, which is home.

The wooded pass, now suffused with the miombo woodlands' September flush of copper-and-gold new leaves, is also known as *Chiramba mumwe*: 'Forbidden to walk alone'.

Tight-throated with mixed anticipation and loss, I feel very much alone.

* * * * *

Epilogue

Starlight

LIKE A loyal fool, I come back.

On the flight into Salisbury that December I find myself sitting next to an RLI major who boasts without pause about cross-border raids and recent 'kills', and curses alike the British toad supervising the new elections, Lord Fuckin Soapy-Soames, the ill-disciplined Security Force Auxiliaries, and the global Communist conspiracy. He says the RLI and my old unit, 4RR, have – at last – 'reamed the ring-piece' out of that old shibboleth of a 'liberated zone', Ngorima. What for? I wonder, when we are just going to hand it back.

'But Mugabe's going to win the next election anyway,' I venture.

'We'll kill the fucker before that, believe you me. Anyway, give them twenty years and they'll fuck it up, just like everywhere in Africa. The white man will be back, you watch.'

I stay silent. I desperately want to shed that racism, the mindset of Them and Us. We are all clearly going to have to transcend those thoughts, or bury them in silence. After three-and-a-half months of hitch-hiking from one stupendous monument of European civilisation to another, the major's rhetoric strikes me as ugly, primitive, and acutely embarrassing.

When we reach the airport he ducks into the gents' and emerges in full military dress-greens, but ends up being shepherded away with apologetic brusqueness by security personnel after he bloodies the nose of a British soldier. Presumably part of the election-monitoring force, the Brit had the gall to proclaim, 'Hullo-'ullo, we've come to win your war for you!'

I get home to the Vumba on Christmas Eve.

At 6 A.M. on Christmas morning I am called out.

It is in effect my first casevac, and the worst thing I ever have to deal with. Just a few k's up the main Vumba road, a Rhodesia Defence Regiment truck, its six or seven occupants none too clearheaded after a night's celebrations, has careered down one of those ferociously steep curves, struck the outer bank, and flipped literally tailpipe over radiator. Two of the soldiers saw the disaster looming and simply jumped overboard, suffering nothing worse than swollen ankles and a few grazes. As my mother and I pull up, they are just easing the driver down from the partially-crushed cab; he is delirious with pain, thrashing a broken upper arm around like a rag toy, his femur gone and the artery pumping blood into the flesh. He has to be calmed with a hard slap, wrestled into sling, tourniquets, splints up to the armpit. Equally worrying are the quiet ones, heads gashed to the bone; I can feel a spine out of alignment, the crepitus of a fractured pelvis. Fortunately, I have swift and competent back-up: a nurse, a couple of Army medics from town in an ambulance. Someone hauls out a bottle of brandy, and is lining up dainty glasses along the tarmac, glinting with incongruous fragility in the early sun.

The injured are finally strapped into stretchers and trucked off to hospital. My mother turns to me, weary and wry:

'Welcome home, son –'

Then rather proudly, '*Starlight.*'

* * *

It is appropriate, in its way, that the main present I have brought back for my father's Christmas is Robert Asprey's monumental history of guerrilla warfare, *War in the Shadows*. Despite everything, warfare, its tactics and technologies, continue to exert an archetypal masculine fascination on both of us. Our own war shows no signs of easing. The radio confides on Christmas evening that three security force personnel, nineteen CTs, and innumerable innocents have been killed that day. What seemed to be a huge hondo going on over Imbeza, with helicopters chuntering, and a Canberra bomber howling overhead, turns out to be a celebratory Christmas flypast.

Celebratory of what, it would be difficult to say.

These are the dying spasms of a closing era. While I was in London, Ian Smith and Abel Muzorewa were there, too, at Lancaster House, finally capitulating to a new constitutional dispensation: a ceasefire followed by an internationally monitored election in which the Patriotic Front of Mugabe and Nkomo, our erstwhile enemies, will participate for the first time. In between haunting the forest, luminous with summer's mingled rain and slanting sun, I diarise our political progress:

27 Dec. *Three British soldiers have been killed in a Puma crash near Mtoko, and a C-130 was fired on west of Umtali, the round entering the aircraft only millimetres from the big white cross on the underside.*

28 Dec. *A group of 300 ZIPRA CTs have refused to accept the cease-fire. There will be a lot of this.*

29 Dec. *The ceasefire started at midnight last night. Patriotic Front forces are gathering at the Assembly Points in 'encouraging' numbers, but there have still been a number of murders and attacks and cross-border incursions of some hundreds. The black parties are already – or should one say 'still' – squabbling, and Nkomo and Mugabe can't agree on whether to fight the election separately or together.*

30 Dec. *Nkomo and Mugabe are to contest the elections separately, which is the best news we've heard yet. It virtually ensures Muzorewa's victory. Soames has deployed small Rhodesian forces along the border to prevent further incursions, which won't help the ceasefire either. The war is going to continue for a fair while yet.*

2 January 1980. *With only two days of the ceasefire to go only 3000-odd PF forces have collected at the Assembly Points. There are still a hell of a lot of violations, including the murder near Penhalonga of Mr Wright from Odzani. Meanwhile the Soviet invasion of Afghanistan and the Iranian shindig are sending the gold price rocketing over $600 an ounce, and the world folds up a little faster than before. Only the Russians and the Rhodesians seem to have any spine left [!].*

4 Jan. *Weirmouth* [near Umtali] *got heavily stonked last night; so much for the ceasefire.*

5 Jan. *The ceasefire officially ended at midnight last night. The monitor-*

ing force says 12000 PF men have assembled; Security Forces say 5000. A swindle going on somewhere. It seems a lot of them are mujibhas, armed with a single dud stick-grenade, sent in while the fighting men stay in the bush. Plenty of bangs today as the Engineers clear the minefield around Forbes Border Post preparatory to opening the border with Mozambique.

So it goes: messy, and out of our control. Our heads are stupefied with anxiety and hope, relief and cynicism, disgust and self-assurance, all in about equal measure. The country we were taught to defend has somehow slipped away, but the country we need to heal is still there, unchanged, harbouring just the same beauties and ills. I continue to finalise my arrangements for university. I write continuously, trying to heal myself through some miraculous act of imagination. I run in the hills with the dogs, barefoot like the child I once was.

Then the registered letters come. The Army is insisting on its final pound of flesh.

* * *

JOC Chipinga swelters under a summer heat at once brazen and humid. Being back in this nerveless camp is reminiscent of my return to Llewellin, the same oppressive desiccation, institutional sediment: the same Pronto, his simian arms and paunch taut as a medicine-ball; the same sloping brown dog; grey buildings hemmed with brown mudsplash; the grey PRAW Cessna on the brown dust apron. At least this time I have the MI Room to myself, to work and sleep in, my nostrils stinging with the multilayered smells of sulphurous medicines.

And on the second day, with a familiarity that feels like a hot hand laid on the back of my neck, a voice grates behind me:

'Jesus, have we got *another* new Starlight?'

It is none other than my old benefactor from Llewellin, the dangerously languid Lieutenant Whorehound.

'Good God, it's The Arm!'

I feel like the tip of the tail in the mouth of the ouroboros, the self-biting serpent whose circle symbolised to the ancients the Unity of Being and Eternal Return.

'You'd better get rid of that horrible fucking beard, Arm, *immediately!*'

But I know my Territorial rights. 'No, thank you, sir.'

'Well, at least do a decent job on my finger, I've just cut it to ribbons carving up your fucking supper.'

'You're working in the *kitchen*, sir?'

'You'll be grateful, you bastard, when you see what you get dished up when I'm not there.'

For a dragging two weeks I languish in that hotbox of an MI Room, like a grub in the bole of a rotting stump. I attend to innumerable trivial complaints, confronted daily by my ignorance, and punch Procillin into the upper-outer-quadrants of countless syphilitic buttocks. One such venereal victim, a general factotum named Magoche, is in the process of receiving maybe the fifth of his ten daily injections when the muscle beneath the needle begins to quiver violently, and he suddenly sways and collapses and starts gibbering deliriously and thrashing about. Thinking he must be having some kind of anaphylactic reaction, I yell for the doctor. The resident doctor is a shy and heavily-bearded Pakistani dubbed Papa Abdul. Papa Abdul lopes over from his quarters, looking incongruous in his unfaded camouflage: he seems always to carry with him, like a ghostly overlay that is more authentic than what he is actually wearing, the aura of a white tarbouch and kaftan. Papa Abdul and I wrestle the jabbering Magoche onto the bed, check his blood-pressure; he gradually comes out of it, intact, but babbling that I had given him poison this time and was clearly attempting to kill him.

But the following day he is back, cheerful, forgiving, and treating me as if there is now some kind of special bond between us. From now on, he will willingly do anything I ask: he is the only man in the camp who will help me mop blood off the floors of the ambulances.

For blood still flows.

One of our star trackers and counter-insurgents, a taciturn Greek ex-Selous Scout, is supplying us fairly regularly with casualties from the Nyanyadzi area. I am first called out when ExSelous reports two CTs wounded in a contact; the choppers are apparently fogged in. Whorehound drives the ambulance down the Chipinga bends at his customary madcap pace, tossing from side to side our second-in-command, a shady-looking Captain Black, and an egg-eyed, mean-mouthed British lieutenant from the Monitoring Force.

The gook, relates ExSelous almost inaudibly, pulled a grenade but they didn't give him the chance even to release the pin. But the chopper *has* flown, and the wounded are gone. We are left with only one body to dispose of.

'The *dogs*,' growls Whorehound.

'We needed the int. from those guys, dammit,' fumes Black. (Black is often giving sly, impromptu pep-talks about how the Security Forces will never let Mugabe win the elections, how there are all sorts of shenanigans going on behind the Monitoring Force's back, how rife intimidation of civilians by the Patriotic Front is, how there are 'contingency plans' to obliterate the Assembly Points, packed with guerrillas, with Frantam, and so on.)

Two days later, ExSelous nails another CT and wounds an un-identified African man; a leg wound, we are told. The 'leg wound' turns out to be an entry-and-exit sucking lung shot: black blood and mucus spits and hisses from the wounds when Papa Abdul lifts the rough field-dressing; we slap on sulfatulle gauze, strap the man down. A couple of times en route to Chipinga I think he is going to die, but he stays half-conscious, moaning softly over and over, '*Maiwe, maiwe, maiwe, maiwe . . .*'. I figure as long as he's vocal he's on the right side of survival.

Then ExSelous comes off with his *pièce de résistance*: a twelve-year-old girl shot through the lower legs, both tibias shattered beyond restoration. We pick her up in the Four-Five ambulance; the local medic has done all the necessary and I have only to see her back to the hospital, change the drip. Magoche is with me, and his shiny black eyes stay fixed on the drip-bulb the whole way, as if it's his own clear life flowing through it. For my part, I am thinking of the girl on the ridge of the Chungwe, the sodden weight of her death in my tugging hands. I wince at every bump as if this new girl's pain were mine. Her pulse continues warm and surprisingly steady. I try to smile at her, but it seems hypocritical. What the hell can she be thinking, the poor mite – if she is thinking at all through the fug of morphine – when one white man in uniform blows her legs away and another one comes in to help her?

A couple of times, over the next few days, I go to see her and other hospital inmates, my heart soggy against my diaphragm. I am only half sealed off by that bedevilling, bred-in impulse not to care overmuch about black people. I write:

> *Here the twelve-year-old sits with her palms up either side of the bandaged thigh stumps. There the old one's lung sucks at the chest-drain, with the pain moaning like a hollow wind in his nostrils. Here there is only one eye looking up, the other is a dull russet orb seeping through the eyepatch. You smile and nod and none smiles back. They are pods, shelled of joy. The ward attendants come and manhandle them ungently to re-dress the wounds; their eyes accuse you, rather, because of your uniform, the colour of your skin, most of all the long rifle pulling at your hand. You run your finger inside your stable-belt, the Medical Corps' red-blue-yellow, touch the black beret tucked in your epaulette, as if that would tell them, tell them you wanted to say, Listen, I'm a medic now, I patched you up, I brought you in here, I don't shoot people any more: this is my volte-face, my atonement.*

But as I look at the downturned face of that girl, wonder what god-awful legless life she will end up living, I am not convinced.

Then I am out of there, clear, gone. Destined for another land, another kind of life, destined not even to vote in the election that Robert Mugabe will win by a landslide, two months hence.

I write about my last journey in a military vehicle:

> *There is a chink of light through the armourplate door, rising dust and blue-black exhaust smoke. Last convoy. The firing-port covers clang down and the rifle muzzles slide out and the slim rounds clash into the breeches. The warm engine vibrates through your seat, you feel the blood pulse in your groin. The trucks growl out. The sun is flattening down on hills of smoky silver, blue, copper, black, you can marvel at the beauty of how it gleams on your rifle barrel, how it fades, how rusty-brown the sky grows. How dark the gold.*
>
> *It is dark. You wait for the ambush, knowing somehow it will never come. You stand then and your head thrusts out into the rushing tunnel of the wind. The road twists out ahead in the headlamps, a dark racing Möbius strip you feel goes on and on forever over the same points. You can feel the corridors of new summer leaves celeb-*

rating, whispering in the dark around you. You can look out beyond it to the blue starlight and beyond that to the great hollow behind, the great black pressure of it. And you know it was more than a mere synastry, a chance reshuffle of time, that brought you through all this.

So desperate I am, then, to salve my experience with some or other metaphor of spiritual meaning, to record the deepest apostasy, even as I try to push it all away from myself into the second-person, even as I recognise that there is no true reversibility, even as I recognise that memories can only be replayed again and again. I know that these events will live alongside, inside, the rest of my life like a strange virus, here hardening arteries and deadening certain nerves, there raking the surface of perceptions to an exquisite tenderness.

* * *

I fire my final round in military service not in anger, but in mercy.

Somewhere along that final journey home, the car up ahead of us skids and stops; they wave us down. One of those skinny little rural mongrels, hardly more than a puppy, has trotted obliviously right under their wheels. Two young girls stand back, looking shocked and transparent in the headlights; their father crouches over it, clasping and unclasping big pale useless hands. The dog's hindquarters are crushed, blood whimpers in bubbles through the panting mouth.

'Don't look,' I say.

But of course they do.

Feeling sick with a black, dizzying emptiness, I blow the puppy's brains out into the earth, and push the little body out into the covering night.

* * * * *

Glossary

Afs	Africans; slightly disparaging
Agric-Alert	farm-based radio network
AMA	(Radio code) African Male Adult
ANC	African National Congress, Ndabaningi Sithole's party (not to be confused with the South African party)
AP	Anti-Personnel
AS	African Soldier
callsign	Radio designation for a 'stick' or place, e.g. 'Four-One-Alpha'
camo	camouflage
casevac	casualty evacuation, either by aircraft or vehicle
chete	(Shona) only, solely, that's all
COIN	Counter-Insurgency
comms	radio communication
Crocodile	armoured personnel carrier; also MAP
CSM	Company Sergeant Major
CT	Communist Terrorist
cuff it	be lazy, do the minimum
doos	(Afrikaans) idiot
doppies	spent cartridge-cases
duzi	(Shona) close by, near
ek sê	(Afrikaans) I say
ES	European Soldier
Fire Force	swift-reaction team of helicopters and paratroopers, sometimes supported by Lynx, Dakota and Canberra aircraft

floppies	guerrillas, allegedly because they 'flopped' when shot
Frantam	napalm-like incendiary bomb
gandanga	(Shona) terrorist; disparaging
gomo	(Shona) hill
gonk; gonk posi	sleep; sleeping spot
graze	food; to eat
HDF	High Density Force
hondo	(Shona) fight, gunfight
hote	(Afrikaans, *houtkop*, wood-head) black person; derogatory
int.	intelligence
JOC	Joint Operations Command
joll	(Afrikaans) have fun; walk jauntily
K-Car	Command or Killer-Car; lead helicopter in Fire Force
katundu	(Shona) kit, baggage
loc; locstat	location, position; map reference for that position
MA2	Medical Assistant, class 2
MA3	Medical Assistant, class 3
Main manna	(Afrikaans) person in charge
MAG	7.62mm heavy machine-gun
MAP	armoured personnel carrier; also Crocodile
MI (room)	Medical Infirmary
mujibha	(Shona) carrier; courier; usually a youngster
mukiwa	(Shona) white person
mull	(Afrikaans, *mal*) crazy
munt	black person; derogatory
mushi	(Shona) nice, lovely
NCO	Non-Commissioned Officer (corporal, sergeant)
ndegi	(Shona) literally, bird; aeroplane
NS	National Service
OP	Observation Post
OSB	Officer Selection Board
penga	(Shona) mad, crazy
PF	Patriotic Front

piccanin	black child
Pronto	(radio code) radio operator
PRAW	Police Reserve Air Wing
PT; PTI	Physical Training; Physical Training Instructor
pull; pulled	shoot; shot
PV	Protected Village
R&R	Rest & Recuperation, holiday; also 'weekend pass'
RAR	Rhodesian African Rifles, almost entirely black unit
rat-pack	ration pack, issued for patrols
RDR	Rhodesia Defence Regiment
rev(ved)	attack(ed)
RF	Rhodesian Front, Ian Smith's ruling party
RIC	Rhodesian Intelligence Corps
RLI	Rhodesian Light Infantry
RMS	Railway Motor Services
RP	Regimental Police
RPD	Russian-made light machine-gun
RSM	Regimental Sergeant Major
RTU	Returned to Unit
RV	rendezvous
SAS	Special Air Service, élite paratroop unit
scant lists	radio code lists
SF	(Rhodesian) Security Forces
shateen	the bush, wilderness
situpa	identification document/pass for black people
sjambok	(Afrikaans) hide whip
Skies	Bulawayo
Sky Pilot	(radio code) priest, pastor
Starlight	(radio code) medic
stick	patrol unit, usually five to seven men
stonk(ed)	attack(ed), usually implying with mortars
Sunray	(radio code) commanding officer
TTL	Tribal Trust Land, area set aside for black people
Two-Five	2.5-ton Unimog truck

UANC	United African National Congress, Abel Muzorewa's party
UDI	Smith's Unilateral Declaration of Independence, 1965
ZANLA	military wing of ZAPU
ZANU	Zimbabwe African National Union, Robert Mugabe's party
ZANU(PF)	ZANU (Patriotic Front), later combination of ZANU and ZAPU
ZAPU	Zimbabwe African People's Union, Joshua Nkomo's party
ZIPRA	military wing of ZAPU
Zookeepers	(radio code) National Parks